Unbinding the Perpetual Soul

Unbinding the Perpetual Soul

Our Human Quest for *Being*

Jeffrey C. Tucker

RESOURCE *Publications* · Eugene, Oregon

UNBINDING THE PERPETUAL SOUL
Our Human Quest for Being

Copyright © 2018 Jeffrey C. Tucker. All rights reserved. Except for brief quotations in critical publications or reviews, no part of this book may be reproduced in any manner without prior written permission from the publisher. Write: Permissions, Wipf and Stock Publishers, 199 W. 8th Ave., Suite 3, Eugene, OR 97401.

Resource Publications
An Imprint of Wipf and Stock Publishers
199 W. 8th Ave., Suite 3
Eugene, OR 97401

www.wipfandstock.com

PAPERBACK ISBN: 978-1-5326-3878-7
HARDCOVER ISBN: 978-1-5326-3879-4
EBOOK ISBN: 978-1-5326-3880-0

Manufactured in the U.S.A.

Dedication

THIS BOOK IS DEDICATED to my Great Aunt Alice Tucker. She was a twentieth century pioneer. A scholar. A creative mathematician. A college teacher and an educator. A writer. An early environmentalist and feminist of sorts. An out-of-the-box thinker. A seeker who was 'spiritual' in the truest and best sense of the word. She could appear outwardly stoic and gruff at times. But always with a purpose. To use these moments as profoundly meaningful learning and coaching ones.

More importantly, she was a mentor to me as I grew up. A friend. A guide. An emotionally stable and 'present' adult who challenged me in my childhood years. And who formed me in ways that she could never have imagined in her wildest dreams. She was not a 'hugger' or demonstrative in her emotions or affection. But her love for me and for my brothers was regularly shown in profound ways beneath the surface. Her care, generosity, and spirit were palpable in all of her actions, even if outwardly hidden in her affect at times. She is gone now and has been for many years. I miss her greatly, but I will always be enormously grateful to her in ways both large and small.

I thank her most of all for urging me not simply to believe or to know. But to also '*seek*'. Not merely to exist. But to also fully '*be*'. Not to idly, passively sit on the sidelines of life. But to also '*quest*' for life in its fullest. Somehow, merely saying 'thank you' doesn't do her profound influence on me sufficient justice. Perhaps writing this book in her honor is a beginning. I hope she'd be pleased.

Contents

Introduction | xi

Prologue: The Quest | 1
Our Quest for Identity | 3
    You-Genic Devolution
    Canary in the Coal Mine
    Inside Out . . . Outside In
    The Invisible Hand
    There's No Place Like Home
    The Gift of Light Within
    'Quest'-ions for Prayer and Further Reflection

Our Quest for Wellbeing | 25
    The Sacred Path of Non-Violence
    Jail Break
    False Promises
    Step Out of Line
    Powerful Near-Sightedness
    The Poetry of Chaos
    'Quest'-ions for Prayer and Further Reflection

Our Quest for Belonging | 43
    Re-Moat-Ly Inhospitable
    Who Loves Me . . . Really?
    The Peace of Deep Listening
    Belonging with an Upbeat Tempo
    The Case For Love
    Salt and Light
    'Quest'-ions for Prayer and Further Reflection

Contents

Our Quest for Truths | 59
- Un-Shelved, Un-Stacked, and Un-Bound
- Deductive Unreality
- This is Not a Test
- On 'Truly' Being
- Out-of-the-Box . . . For a Change
- Guess Who's Coming To Dinner
- 'Quest'-ions for Prayer and Further Reflection

Our Quest for Things Sacred | 80
- Burning the Bridges Behind You
- The 'Ark' of the Covenant
- 'Above' the Iceberg
- 'Dislocated' Space . . . 'Found' Hope
- Prayer as 'Reflexive'
- Sharing the Sacred Together
- 'Quest'-ions for Prayer and Further Reflection

Our Quest for Healing | 97
- Solitary Confinement
- Wrestling with God
- What Kind of a God are You, Anyway?
- Freedom Through Forgiveness
- A Call to 'Arms' . . . And Legs
- Closure: Trusting the Source
- 'Quest'-ions for Prayer and Further Reflection

Our Quest for Transcendence | 115
- Manifest Destiny
- Immersion Conversion
- Salvation Story at the 'Cross'-Roads
- Engaging a Faint Voice
- Welcome to the Family
- Extraordinary Revelation
- 'Quest'-ions for Prayer and Further Reflection

CONTENTS

Our Quest for Meaning | 139
    Seemingly Contradictory
    The Exact Time Is . . .
    Shifting Sand . . . Shifting Time
    The Joy Beneath the Surface
    Revolutionary Change
    Re-Awakening our Inner Child
    'Quest'-ions for Prayer and Further Reflection

Epilogue: The Quest | 163
With Infinite Gratitude | 164

Introduction

Quest

- *To search for something important*
- *To pursue in order to find*
- *To actively seek something hidden*
- *A challenging expedition or journey taken to secure or achieve a thing*
- *An expression of a need or desire for something*

WHAT IF OUR ACTUAL lives aren't 'written' like a simple story? Nor like a book that flows neatly and sequentially from 'chapter-to-chapter' via a rigidly linear plot. And isn't populated by highly scripted characters. And doesn't end in uninspiring, predictable ways. But written, instead, through a series of creative interludes or moments. Further still, what if our lives shouldn't simply happen *to* us? Shouldn't act on us externally. Or be imposed on us from the outside by circumstances beyond our control. Or randomly occur with neither rhyme nor reason. But, rather, lived by our own affirmative acts of seeking 'life'. And doing so with the entirety of our human beings. As part of an ongoing, active pursuit. Done in sustained and purposeful ways.

Seeking 'life' in this way is not reacting to what may come. It's not an unconscious response to what may happen to us. It's not simply accepting the inevitable with resignation or even grace. No. Seeking life demands a choice by us. It requires a profound, transformational choice, at that. We do this when we choose to no longer simply 'exist'. To no longer abide in another's rules or expectations. To no longer feel judged in a game of another's choosing. We do this when we actively choose to reject the holy grail of

Introduction

human progress, as it is currently understood: our achievements, earnings, possessions, conquests, and even our transient 'happiness'. It happens when we choose to actually live for a change. And, in so doing, to venture out. To seek uncharted things and undiscovered places. To begin a 'quest'. A human quest for deeply spiritual lives of continuously 'becoming'. A courageous, rewarding act of 'lived' redemption.

However, in order to quest, we must *first* unbind our souls. Unbind our seemingly perpetual souls that we've slowly, incrementally layered onto ourselves along the way. Like heavy, course scales with the hardness of plated armor. Bound tightly in ways that feel protective. But, in truth, constituting a thick skin that chokes out our very breath and light within. In order to unbind our souls, though, we must sometimes 'unlearn' many of the things we've previously been taught. The very things that we've consciously or unconsciously appended onto and into our very beings. Then consider the notion that the human act of seeking truths is the only real truth in an actively spiritual life.

Doing this doesn't mean that all things are relative. It doesn't mean that each of us is left to define 'truth' for ourselves in selfish, self-serving ways. Or that we should use our respective 'truths' to squash, to marginalize, or to overpower other people in the process. A life of seeking is *not* that. Instead, it's a continuous, purposeful quest for the things that actually make us human. We become more human when we discern our own purpose in living. When we stay open to different perspectives, however challenging and provocative they might initially appear to us.

Further, we become more human when we hold far less tightly to that which we're told to believe. When we ask more openly curious, thoughtful, and probing questions. When we see all 'truths' in the specific, unique contexts and agendas of their respective authors. Then ask whether they make sense in our own situations. Finally, we become more human when we ask if the 'truths' that we hold closest are actually working for us. Ask if they're truly helping us to cope, grow, and spiritually flourish. In the end, we become more human only when we first 'unbind' our souls. When we unbind ourselves.

However, we must do so much more than that. For if we stop at 'unbinding', we discount the possibility of any universal truths. In effect, we embark on a path of utterly unstructured human relativism. A path of giving ourselves wholly to our uncensored whims, desires, sense of formless spontaneity, or even chaos. As such, nothing of lasting value is gained

Introduction

by merely 'dumping our bound-up baggage' if it all ends there. The payoff comes when, and only when, we do something with what remains. With our now unbound souls. When we actually take the quest.

Our quests are quite transcendent. They're existential and 'spiritual' in nature. They subsume our religious beliefs, although we can be both religious and spiritual simultaneously so long as we appreciate the important differences involved. We can hold both denominational faith beliefs and the 'spirit of the quest' at the same time . . . provided that we're open, not guarded and possessive, in that faith. That said, taking the quest for 'being' goes much farther than simply dogma. It demands our openness, our spirit of continuous seeking, our inward curiosity, and our focus on broad principles for living.

Our quests therefore transcend not just our religions, our held dogmas, and our sacraments of faith. They encompass *all* spheres of our human 'beings'. These quests influence our beliefs—about our origins, other beings, our world, our universe, God, and ourselves. Further, they help to form our thinking. On how we conceptualize and connect things, create new ideas, make sense of the past, and muse on the future. Our quests also support our ability to truly feel—to name, articulate, and more fully express our deepest feelings.

But that's not all. Questing informs our actions, whether solving problems, making judgments and decisions, prioritizing things, or successfully completing life's many tasks. Lastly, it acts in concert with our relating to others. In how we communicate, function in groups and families, provide and receive support, and respond to change. In other words, it's impossible to separate our respective quests from ourselves as human beings.

Those brave enough to undertake a quest seek many things. With souls unbound, we quest for identity and wellbeing. We seek belonging. We pursue truths. The search for all things sacred, wherever they may be found. We quest for healing. We seek transcendence. And we pursue the very meanings of our lives. Our real, truest purposes for being here. The existential 'groundings' of our existence. And we seek these things not through some step-by-step process. Not in accord with any single source, book, or guide. Not via some linear and sequential chapter-to-chapter progressive narrative. But through trial and error. Through persistence. In the very midst of life's inevitable struggles. With heart and with soul.

Thus the format of this book. As you'll soon discover, I write *Unbinding the Perpetual Soul* as a series of creative essays, not as a continuous

Introduction

narrative. For our lives and our quests are not lived in traditional narrative ways. The twists, turns, sources of insights, unexpected developments, and resultant human growth that we experience each day are more akin to 'essays' than a simple story. The reality of our lives demands that we integrate the seemingly incongruous, the unrelated, the less-than-obvious, and the unanticipated. This reality requires that we're willing to be challenged. To engage with new, even provocative, ideas. To draw on a variety of sources. Then form our own paths as we go. While, at the same time, staying open to 'un-forming' and 're-forming' these paths as new insights arise.

That's the nature of a quest. It's not an easy journey, to be sure. But it's life changing. It's exhilarating. It's exciting and rewarding. And while far from certain in its destination, one thing is for sure: you'll be a better, healthier, and far more actualized person in the process. You'll be more spiritually 'whole' and grounded. So join me on this quest, if you will. An inclusive, soulful, unbinding one. A life-giving and life-sustaining human quest for being.

Prologue: The Quest

We are given Life in order to experience true life.
We're given the Divine in order to seek the Divine.
We're given our Capacity in order to find that of divinity within us.
We're given our Gifts in order to discern what is possible.
We're given our Hearts in order to love the unknowable.
We're given our Eyes in order to see the unrecognizable.
We're given our Minds in order to dream the unthinkable.
We're given our Hands in order to sculpt the improbable.
We're given our Feet in order to trek the impassable.
And our Souls in order to do the undoable.
Thank you, Loving Creator God, for it all.

Our Quest for Identity

Identity:

- *A thing or person's existence*
- *An essential part of something or someone*
- *One's personhood*
- *The distinguishing essence of oneself*
- *That which actually is*

You-Genic Devolution

EUGENICS IS THE SCIENCE of enhancing our genetic quality as people. It focuses on maximizing the human qualities or traits believed to be desirable or undesirable. In some of its practice historically, it worked to foster the procreation of those deemed as having 'good qualities'. Conversely, it discouraged reproduction of people deemed 'bad' by those with the power to decide these things. Procreation by 'undesirables' was dissuaded or prevented by marriage restrictions, forced abortions, and mandatory sterilizations. Those deemed inferior included the mentally challenged, the emotionally afflicted, the poor and uneducated, and those of marginalized ethnicities and races.

These weeding-out eugenics practices were accepted and even encouraged by many in the mainstream, continuing well into the 20th century. Perhaps eugenics was seen as a way to hasten, improve, or 'juice-up' Darwin's Theory of Evolution. Darwinism proposed that all living things evolve in ways that weed-out those who are less able to survive and thrive in the world. A process of natural selection works to favor living things that are fittest to compete and to win.

Eugenics theories and practices assume that we successfully evolve through public policies, practices, or the invisible hand of nature ... however draconian they may be. The thrust is unmistakably 'forward'—driving humanity to a greater, stronger, smarter, and more robust future. But what if the forces of evolution, however arbitrary or draconian, are being thwarted by yet another force in the world today? What if humanity is willingly and wittingly embarking on a track of *Devolution*? A path of going backwards in our human processes of critical thinking, expression, and decision-making. And, unlike the sinister forces of eugenics, this time we're doing it to ourselves: *You-Genics*.

In author Neil Postman's book, *Amusing Ourselves to Death*, he boldly painted our potential future as one in which we've voluntarily and blissfully dulled our senses and brains through incessantly entertaining ourselves into oblivion. On the way to this oblivion, we've effectively removed ourselves from the 'public squares' of logic, reason, and informed civil discourse. In so doing, we've abdicated our role as rational, informed participants in society. We've done so in favor of entertainment and distraction in our lives. And we've become less human in our identity as a result.

What makes our current *You-Genic Devolution* so frightening is the speed and magnitude of its practices in our society today. Even more sinister is our willingness to blithely walk the path of ignorance with nary a second thought. Of course, the retardation of our brains is nicely helped along by external forces. Freedom of thoughtful expression is thwarted in many cultures of fear, secrecy, and repression. The number of independently owned, community based media outlets is rapidly shrinking—replaced by far fewer regional, national, or global conglomerates located far from the trenches of the reporting localities.

This ominous consolidation of media power necessarily limits the range of informed opinions and viewpoints available to us. As if to make this even worse, national cable news in the United States is increasingly advocacy-based, not news and journalism-centered. TV and on-line news networks have stated political agendas. And they use their 24-hour per day platforms to espouse their respective party lines. We often tune into these 'news' outlets because we *already* agree with their points of view. In turn, our preexisting views are continuously reinforced in our minds. We're not intellectually stretched. Instead, we're retarded, cemented and encased.

On the local front, newscasts routinely report crimes, fires, natural disasters, and entertainment rumors. Not because they believe these stories to be important in a 'macro' sense. But because they're visual. They titillate our senses and appeal to our carnal instincts. Further, news stories, more generally, are increasingly 'dumbed-down'. They're presented in short, pithy, and superficial ways, tailored nicely to our equally short attention spans and to our limited knowledge of the subjects involved. Finally, many of us regularly eschew the insights and wonders of the arts, history, and sciences for the rough-and-tumble of sports, sit-coms, and reality shows. Not just once in a while for escape. But regularly in the spirit of habitual escapism.

On a personal level, we're purposefully thwarting our innate capacity around curiosity, learning, writing, and thoughtful discourse. Social and political matters are spouted and spewed, not rationally debated in informed ways. Ideas and substance wilt in the crossfire of talking points and venom. In the process, critical ideas are sterilized in short, terse tweets. Logic becomes lazy. Pre-programmed beliefs and lethargic logic vanquish facts and data. We withdraw into our shrinking brains. Increasingly isolated. Sadly, we also shrink in the face of mass commercialization. In our desire to be entertained rather than to be informed, we become nothing more than manipulated objects of corporate and organizational branding.

It's possible that many will argue this point, calling out our ongoing attempts to remain in this world rather than dulling our minds. But as my aforementioned depiction of our slow demise is protested, some tough questions might be in order. For example, what have we read of any real substance during the last few months or years? What do we actually watch on TV and how much do we tune in each day? When was the last time that we wrote something of substantive content and import? When we posted something insightful to our journals? When we wrote a thoughtful letter to our elected officials? And how much do we understand or even care about current events in our area, state, nation, and the world?

There are more questions for us, as well. How civically informed are we? Can we name our Congress person, US Senators, and Governor? Can we rationally explain the basis for our own party affiliations in our voting? Or discuss with some substance the specific issues that drive these voting patterns? Are we actually involved in issues that we purport to have some passion about—beyond merely writing a check to financially contribute once in a while? How is the world a better place because of what we've said or accomplished in our lives beyond the workplace and our daily jobs?

Yet even more questions. Are we surrounding ourselves with diverse people of different opinions in a purposeful effort to listen to other viewpoints, learn from them, and stretch ourselves along the way? How much time are we spending on social media each day, and to what end? And what are we modeling to our children and grandchildren about making wise, informed choices with our discretionary time, talents, and capacity to grow? The answers that we give to *all* these questions might surprise us. In a devolutionary kind of way, if you know what I mean. You-Genetics. What we're voluntarily doing to ourselves.

The history of human eugenics has a dark chapter to it. A program of forced weeding-out and sterilization in order to create a superior product. Decided by others. How ironic is it, then, that we're currently sterilizing ourselves by *reducing* our capacity to think and to grow? If someone from another planet happens alongside an earthly human being a few hundred years from now, who and what will they encounter? Will they find us in our caves, intellectually bereft, groggy, and dull? Or will they see a better, engaged, and invested public—with a strong sense of identity working hard to make the world a better place for all? It's a question worth pondering.

Do we really want to go quietly into the night in a self-medicated, sedated, and anesthetic bliss? Do we want to reduce our lives to the least-common denominator? Sometimes the simplest solution isn't the right one. The real answer lies in the complicated nuance of things. Sometimes paddling upstream is worth the effort. Spiritual growth and the positive evolution of our identities as human 'beings' require our disciplined training. Demand our hard work. Our sweat and toil. And we have to actively and purposefully choose the better path.

For we have a choice, to be sure. We have this choice because God has given us the ability to choose. We can choose to reduce our human, intellectual dimensions to 'one'. We can devolve into one-dimensional or even identity-void creatures. Alternatively, we can fight back. We can add dimensions. Add layers. Add richness. And add color and texture. We can go forward, not backwards. Evolve, not devolve. You can decide. We can decide. If only we wake up before it's too late.

Canary in the Coal Mine

The Apostle Paul was a prolific, foundational, and highly influential author of many books in the 2nd Testament of the Bible. Paul was a 1st Century theologian, writer, guide to pastoral life, and thinker on how early Christians might best worship Jesus. Paul was also a Jew and a Roman citizen. As 'Saul', Paul had previously persecuted the believers of the risen Christ. He had sought them out in order to bring them to Jerusalem for trial and punishment for their heresy.

That was the case until he saw a light from Heaven on the road to Damascus. And heard the risen Christ's voice. Asking Saul why he was persecuting Jesus. As the story goes, the post-resurrection Christ chose Saul (who later became Paul) to be the vehicle through which Christ's name might be shared with Gentiles and with others. In many ways, it was an unusual and unlikely choice. But Paul responded mightily, helping to 'seed', nurture, and sustain a multitude of new believers in Christ. Paul was persecuted in the process of so doing. He was imprisoned. Schemed against. And ultimately executed in Rome, according to most believers. Many hold that his greatest contribution was in establishing the nascent Christian 'church' and fostering its subsequent growth.

While Paul was an unquestionably deep theological thinker, he was also infinitely practical. His Epistles in the 2nd Testament are quite situational—targeted to specific issues and problems that believers were facing at the time. His focus was on how these believers could act in ways glorifying the Risen Christ while they anxiously awaited their own resurrection as part of Christ's coming return. Paul talked very little, in fact, about Christ as living, incarnational savior: Christ's actual life. This makes some sense, as Paul never knew Jesus while he was alive on this earth. Paul undoubtedly learned about that life from Christ's disciples. But Paul knew Jesus as solely a post-resurrection light and voice.

The Apostle Paul's frame of reference, therefore, was not in Christ's time as a living, breathing human. Not in God in the flesh as Jesus. But in the risen Savior. The Way. But it's an erroneous leap of faith to draw a resultant conclusion that Paul's sole focus was on our spiritual 'souls' in Christ. That Paul ignored the import of Christ's life. Or simply glossed over the 'earthy and fleshy' practicalities and respective contexts of our own lives as followers of Jesus. To appreciate this fully, we have to approach Paul in his own context and in his own time. Specifically, for purposes of this essay, in the context of civic and religious 'law'.

Paul was a Roman citizen. And he was well acquainted with the practical protection that his political citizenship (and the associated laws surrounding it) afforded him. In fact, Paul wisely used this Roman law on occasion to his own advantage when persecuted. As a practicing Jew, Paul *also* knew well the importance of strict observance of religious ritual (law) in Jewish life. He stood in good company on that score. For even Jesus didn't reject 'the law' of the Jewish people. Jesus said that he came to actually fulfill it. All of it. In its truest spirit. So Paul's onslaughts against the 'law' in the Bible's 2nd Testament weren't, in all probability, a total rejection of it.

As such, what if the 'law' that Paul so ardently rejected was the *complicity of religious and political law taken together*? By this, I mean the collusion practiced between the province of Judea and Rome. Under Rome's client kings (and Roman rule) within the province, Jews were permitted to practice their faith in Judea. But they were also largely controlled by Rome. Controlled by Rome's power to threaten. To punish. To control militarily. And to tax. Paul knew this well. As a Roman citizen and a Jew, he knew. He would, therefore, have preached the Word of Christ and ministered at some real personal risk for his very life.

So, a lot was at stake for Paul in the highly combustible climate of Rome's power. Given this, the real problem with the law for Paul might not have been in its strictly spiritual sense. But instead as it regarded the legal collusion between already established religious beliefs and the political power of the Roman Empire. Paul's appeal to reject the 'law' was thus not just religious, but political and practical as well. And this rejection came at a real cost to Paul.

As a 'blinding voice and light' on the road to Damascus, Jesus promised Saul (later Paul) that Saul would endure persecution for his work. He would experience personal suffering. Just like Jesus did. For Christ had previously 'called out' the risks of this very same church/state collusion while he was on earth. This collusion cost Christ his life. In turn, Paul's greatest contribution may have been his work in continuing Christ's own words. Precautionary warnings of things to come. Like the Canary in the Mineshaft smelling deadly vapors on the way into the abyss.

Most Christians celebrate the founding of the institutional church. Constantine I of Rome was 'converted' before he died. In the 4th Century, he made Christianity the only recognized faith in the Empire. How ironic that the government replaced its own state 'religion' with the very one it had so ardently persecuted during the preceding centuries. For some, this signaled the joyful beginning of the institutional Christian church, as we know it today. I would respectfully argue otherwise.

Our Quest for Identity

For in making Christianity a state-sponsored religion, the very essence of Christ's message would slowly dissipate over time. Our very identities as people of faith would be subsumed. Jesus must have known this. For he never called for the formation of a 'church', per se. In fact, he only mentioned the word 'church' a few times in the 2nd Testament of the Bible. While these sayings do address notions of organizing believers in some fashion, it's unlikely that Christ had an institutional plan in mind. Not, at least, as we can realistically discern by reading the Bible.

To the contrary, Christ was far more interested in the spirit and heart of believers: their truest identities as spiritual people. He knew all too well from his own life about the dangers of protecting the institution of religion on the backs of its believers. And the hypocrisy and even violence that can result from it. Given this, the early Christian church before Constantine rightly modeled what Christ had in mind. Doing 'church' was generally comprised of small gatherings of people in private homes. Admittedly, they did share some common elements of worship, practice, and practical leadership. But believers gathered for the most part in loosely structured, informal communities.

To this very point, most followers of the nascent Christian faith believed that Christ was returning very soon—perhaps in their very lifetimes. It's therefore doubtful that they over-engineered the practices of their faith. There wouldn't be time to do so and it didn't really matter given the short time span ahead. But things changed dramatically in this regard when these communities subsequently assumed the regal trappings of the 'church'. And not for the better. Paul must have instinctively known that it would happen. He was Christ's Canary in the Coal Mine. He tried to tell us. But we were busy doing 'church'.

And we know how it all turned out in history. Without question or debate, Christian churches have done some marvelous things. In many important ways, the world is far better for them. But, throughout our history, our church institutions have *also* colluded with and seized secular power. Constantine started it. In the later period of the Middle Ages, the church became a land-owning and wealthy entity. Strict tithing was akin to onerous taxation on church members. Church leaders held onto rigid authority to interpret the Bible to a largely illiterate peasant population. Indulgences were sold in order to enact forgiveness. And to ensure the heavenly repose of 'sinners' and their families. Churches held the power to excommunicate, try, imprison, and even execute 'heretics'.

With the subsequent onset of the Reformation, the notion of 'Royal Authority' emerged. And this royal authority now simultaneously became religious authority. A Constantine Roman version of sorts . . . revisited. Kings became heads of respective churches. Religious civil wars were fought. Intolerance of other faiths grew. Religious inquisitions fostered fear, torture, intrigue, and reporting of those persons suspected of having 'fallen away'. And as history progressed, churches gave 'passes' to questionable secular rulers. And visa versa.

For example, far too many church leaders failed to actively condemn 20th Century tyrants such as Hitler and Mussolini. They utterly failed to adequately protest the horrific and deadly anti-Semitic policies and practices of these killers. Conversely, and more recently in history, too many secular (and religious) institutions have, for all intents and purposes, actively colluded to provide cover for some in church positions who've perpetrated atrociously abusive, unspeakable, and criminal acts towards innocent people both young and old. Countless lives and souls have been lost as a result.

Given the aforementioned broad sweep of history, what actually happens when church and state collude? When formal, institutional religions are unreasonably influenced by a government or a Crown? When the survival and growth of an organized religious belief system tries to influence elective, political, or governmental processes or policies? When it happens, the basic principles of religious life and human identity become intolerably enmeshed within the 'rough and tumble' of secular politics. The power of government is used to enforce the beliefs of the predominant religion. To fight dissent regarding those beliefs. To imprison dissenters. To impose these beliefs on the population as a whole.

Further, when collusion happens, it creates zealous, rigid societal restrictions—effectively constricting and limiting the rights to worship otherwise and elsewhere. Sometimes quite subtly. But always convincingly. For the power of 'going along' is palpable to be sure. Perhaps most importantly, though, institutional religion (when coupled too closely with political power) is corrupted. From the outside and from the inside. One side compromises for the other. It's a mutual selling-out process. Worse yet, it separates us from each other. Sublimating the things that we have in common in favor of things that artificially separate us. And it's undermining our very individual identities. This isn't spiritual in any sense of the word. In fact, it's existentially suffocating.

Our Quest for Identity

Jesus Christ's tomb lies under and within the Church of the Holy Sepulcher in the Middle East. Part of the Christian sector of the Old City portion of Jerusalem. The Old City historically comprises multiple 'quarters'– those for Christians, Armenians, Jews, and Muslims, respectively. The Church of the Holy Sepulcher is, itself, shared by multiple Christian sects. The site of Christ's actual tomb is breathtaking. The actual church is said to sit on the sites of Christ's passion, crucifixion, and burial in a then-standing cave. The church is also situated within the larger environment of a city considered holy to Christian, Jewish, and Muslim religions. Contested, in fact. Fought over in history. Multiple times.

I often wonder what Christ thinks about the place in which his tomb still survives. One that is visited by multitudes of peoples each day. And venerated. And protected as if the place is supposed to be religiously set-apart and sacred. While it simultaneously sits within a city (and region) where blood has been needlessly and abundantly spilled over the organized practices of religions through history. Where politics and policies and power and 'might' have readily mixed with religious beliefs in such combustible ways since his death and burial. The fact that Christ isn't actually lying in the tomb should tell us something. He may have foreseen the future as he rose from the tomb on that Easter morning some two thousand years ago. He might, even now, lament what his movement has evolved into during the many centuries that have followed.

Jesus Christ is likely to mourn the fact that we probably missed the whole point of his coming in the first place. We've lost the forest for the trees, in fact. And have failed to truly hear his message. Then subsequently failed to hear Paul's message. Or partially misinterpreted it in the interest of building a 'church' instead of a movement or a collective spiritual identity. In so doing, we've failed to heed the warnings of the canary: of Jesus, then Paul. The Canary in the Coal Mine. That was trying to tell us: "Stop this before it's too late. Before faith and spirituality are lost forever in some colluded, state-protected religion."

Perhaps a canary isn't even the best metaphor here. Maybe a dove does it more justice. For a dove embodies the idea of peace. Embodies the power of the Spirit and the Spiritual. Of purity of love, not rigid beliefs. Of innocence. Of the freedom of flight. Not imprisonment of the heart. Perhaps it's not too late to save the canary from the mineshaft—as long as the bird is still living. The dove is doing its best. To breathe for the canary. Until we pull that battered canary out of the mine. And give it its life back. Give us our own lives back, for that matter. And, in the process, restore our truest, non-colluded identities. Jesus knew it. Paul did too. We should, as well.

Inside Out . . . Outside In

There's no end to theories that try to explain how we develop our human identities. About what governs our behaviors, choices, and actions as adults. Some theorists believe that we act out of pent-up, unconscious, and unmet sexual needs and fantasies dating back to our earlier lives as infants, toddlers, and adolescents. Others argue that we all go through various developmental stages as part of growing older. In the process, some get stunted at times– while others progress more steadily.

That's not all. For yet another group of theorists argues that we're grounded in essential personality types. These innate characteristics govern our choices throughout our lives. A few would go so far as to argue that we're inherently programmed by our internal instincts. Like rats in a maze, it's all about our learning the specific behaviors that get us the prize. In the case of the rats, it's always the cheese. Some of us like cheese, as well, I imagine.

While the development of our human identities is far more nuanced than any one theory would have us believe, I am 'partial' to *Social Learning Theory*. One of its principal thinkers, Julian Rotter, argued that human behavior is most influenced by one's social context, environmental factors, and the rational process of human learning– not by internal psychological or physiological considerations. Rotter believed that our behavior is based, first and foremost, on the expected outcome or effect of that specific behavior. By the likelihood of this outcome. And by our own perception of that outcome's desirability.

More positive and likely outcomes are associated with higher levels of our human motivation to act in ways that bring this outcome about—as well as repeating this behavior in the future. Behavior happens, therefore, not instinctually or based on our unconscious internal drive—but more so by virtue of our interactions with our external environments as individuals. These interactions are fluid, responding to changes in our environment, our perceptions of those changes, and our learning from our past experiences. Each of us is unique and different inasmuch as we experience, interpret, and learn in different ways in response to our respective contexts and our own individual needs.

An important element of Julian Rotter's thinking was *Locus of Control*. He argued that each of us carries sets of beliefs (however rational or irrational) about the primary determinants of our success in achieving desired outcomes with the greatest likelihood. Those of us with an *internal* locus of control believe that desired outcomes are achieved and maximized by our own internal efforts. Success lies primarily within us. Conversely, those driven by an *external* locus of control believe that achieving desired results is driven principally by random chance, luck, or the influence or power of others. External locus of control thinkers tend to view their own agency as having minimal, if any, impact.

Whatever our locus of control orientation is, we tend to slowly and incrementally learn it over time as our actions are continuously reinforced by our perception of the reality and contexts around us. We learn and internalize our locus and our expectations early on in life. We're conditioned by what we've been taught at home, on the streets, in school, in church, on the job, and even in play. We learn to think, value, expect, and act in accordance with our unique environments. Even our intrinsic needs, which drive our expectations and moderate our reinforcement values, are in many ways modeled and taught to us. In some ways, then, we're all products of things external to us. In some cases, even more so than on our own intrinsic identities, souls, and internal compasses.

There is, perhaps, a no more visible place to 'study' this theory than in people in identity crises: whether from illness, loss, trauma, isolation, substance abuse, or troubled relationships. In far too many cases, people's ability to process these crises in healthier, more effective ways is hampered by their prior conditioning. In short, by what they've already learned and have had continuously reinforced. Too many people have experienced sexual, physical, and emotional abuse while growing up within their families of origin.

Many were simultaneously raised in families modeling drug or alcohol abuse or dependence by their parents. Others grew up in families fractured by conflict, estrangement, or neglect. Conversely, some people came from fairly stable homes, only to be thrust into military service overseas. They returned home utterly broken by the loss of their very souls and their 'beings' in warfare—experiencing the traumas of lost lives, the killing of others, fracturing of values and beliefs, heavy guilt, loss of self-identity, and learned behaviors that are now ill-suited for successful transition back into peacetime living stateside.

In yet other situations, people grapple with depression and have seriously contemplated suicide with regularity. Some have attempted it. Some have tried multiple times. Some have not yet tried, but face suicidal ideation for the first time. And others have physically cut themselves in the form of small daily mutilations to their arms, legs, or hands. Many are alcohol or drug dependent—or are in a bumpy and often sporadic process of recovery.

Sadly, the common denominator in far too many of these situations is a learned, enormously strong External Locus of Control. In keeping with this locus of their identities, people feel overwhelmed and paralyzed by outside 'forces'. They often have little support from family and have few functionally healthy friends. Their resources are typically quite minimal. Further, most often they've learned a low sense of self. They find affirming or even describing themselves very difficult. They feel utterly disempowered.

They find no time for such things as insights, self-fulfillment, or actualization. They strive primarily for safety and the basics of their next meal, staying warm at night, finding shelter, and securing any work that they feel capable of doing. The blank stare in their eyes is haunting to me when, in my past work as a Chaplain, I have asked them 'who *they* are'. They simply don't know in many cases. They've learned not to care anymore. They've become victims of the ongoing reinforcement of their own low expectations.

Social Learning Theory is, therefore, quite powerful as a guide to how humans develop their respective identities. However, no single way of seeing ourselves as spiritual human 'beings' is complete in and of itself. Perhaps my greatest critique regarding Social Learning Theory lies in its tendency to wholly underestimate the inherent existence of the sacred, guiding spark of light and goodness within each of us. It risks placing far too much emphasis on our external environment and our adaptation to it.

In so doing, this theory also risks reducing our lives and our beings to an exercise of learned behaviors. I fear that this makes us less whole and less spiritually integrated in our identities as a result. Sadly, it therefore makes us less human. It can also make us perpetual 'victims'—living life in ways that consciously or unconsciously sabotage our true selves as we learn to simply respond rather than to self-empower. It takes away our inherent 'agency' for our own lives.

To be fair now, our contexts, upbringing, and adaptation *do* matter. They have something important to add to the equation of our behaviors and our development, to be sure. But it doesn't end there. And what if there's a better way? What if we live not simply by learning new behaviors or raising our expectations? Instead we live, as well, when we reconnect with the inherently unique and special persons that God created us to be from the outset. Right down to the core of our very souls. To the core of our unique identity as spiritual people.

As such, our development is not simply an *Outside-In* equation. What we learn can be unlearned with some effort when our prior learning isn't spiritually helpful to us. In other words, we can change. We can re-create ourselves with God's loving help. Given this, we develop in an *Inside-Out* way, as well. Not as part of some programmed scheme, though. Not encased within a theory or model. But via a creative, transformative process of human spiritual growth. For each of us is special and different. No two of us are fully alike. We're unique in our respective identities as persons. Created that way. *Inside-Out . . . and Outside-In.*

The Invisible Hand

Adam Smith was an 18th Century economist and moral philosopher. He's credited with developing the theory of the 'Invisible Hand', although he didn't explicitly use this language in his writings. Smith argued that our respective actions in pursuing individual benefits actually accrue to the greater benefit of the whole society in the end. This is because our work, however self-centered it is in its intent, strives to produce the greatest value and distinction—which, in turn, benefits others in the wider world even if unintentionally so.

It's as if an invisible hand uses our efforts toward a greater good in spite of ourselves. And in spite of our own motives. Smith's theory is analogous, in some ways, to the more current nomenclature around the 'trickle-down economy'. According to this thinking, individual wealth and prosperity ultimately find their way into the hands of the many. Even though a significant portion of that wealth stays with the individual, some of it ultimately trickles down to the masses for more generalized benefit. Everybody wins in the end. So individual wealth creation should be encouraged, no matter how concentrated it appears to be on the surface.

However they might rationalize away the ongoing concentration of individual wealth, these theories, in actual truth, only 'muddy the waters' by blurring the important distinction between that which benefits the few versus that which benefits the many. And the theories encourage our worst instincts: that, left to our own devices, humans will do the right thing for others in the final analysis—no matter their original intent. As spiritual people, our intent *does* matter, though. In our quests for identity, our intent does matter. It matters irrespective of the probable or even possible outcomes of our actions.

But intent is not the whole story. The locus of benefits actually received matters as well. Many ancient societies, and even a few today, did and still do focus primarily on the welfare of the *entire* community versus the rights of the individual. These communities value the sacred nature of the 'family'. As a result, the rights of the few must defer to the good of the whole in certain instances. The whole is greater than the sum of the individual parts. And this amounts to a guiding, grounding, foundational spiritual virtue.

The spiritual virtue of 'communion people' lives today where shared values and principles ascend to a level of prominence in the daily lives of people. Where these values guide individual choices in all nature of things. Where love is the principal end to be sought. It's possible that societal or familial norms engrain this in the lives of community members. It's possible that these virtues are taught to each new generation from childhood. It's also possible, though, that these societies are simply following their own inherent moral compass. They're 'listening to' their already-existing relational DNA inside their very souls. The genes that God placed in their hearts as part of creation.

But here's the problem: not all societies listen to their souls. Seemingly few do these days, in fact. Does this necessarily mean that only a few of us have these genes inside us? That God gave the 'community DNA' to only a few? I think not. We *all* have it inside of us. Sadly, however, most of us fail to follow our own hearts. We fail to do so because the larger society works so diligently against doing so. For it's hard to listen closely when our souls' heartbeats are drowned out. Drowned out by the multitudes that preach otherwise so effectively and prominently. Obscured by the deafening sound of yet another message: we must win at all costs. Winning should be valued over all else. The end justifies the means, whenever necessary.

If that's not enough, our own fears hinder us, as well. Especially when we're subject to constant rumblings of daily fear mongering—ironically enough, by institutions that have a significant stake in our hunkering down ever more deeply. When this happens, we unwittingly partner in protecting the very institutions that are corrupting our souls. A kind of Stockholm Syndrome, if you will.

Next, our loving, sharing DNA is incrementally sapped from our souls when we're constantly desensitized to the humanity of others. When we're taught to see others as somehow less-than-human. As objects, not as people. And our capacity to think 'whole versus what's mine' is hindered by our distance from others. When we separate from family, friends, or the world more broadly, we get farther away from their needs. However wittingly or unwittingly, we lose touch. First with others. Then with ourselves and with our identities. In an era of unparalleled 'connectivity', we're turning increasingly inward—buried beneath the protective screens of our smart phones, pads, and laptops. It's hard to truly value community when it's only experienced virtually.

Lastly, and ironically enough, we lose our loving, sharing genes when we continue to rigidly obey the strict rules of accepted living. To be honest, following rules is easy. It's much harder to live in accord with shared values grounded in love. For following values (versus rules) means that we have to think and discern. To make trade-offs. To compromise. To share. To see others as our equals. To hold their hands. To help them up. To hold the whole together. Sometimes even at our own individual cost.

So our own inherent 'communal' DNA is blunted in numerous ways in our world. To be sure. Pushed aside by any number of things that work so mightily to dull our souls, our humanity, and our communities of true 'being' together. As such, it's easy to blame the outside world. However, the outside world isn't the biggest contributor here. As it turns out, the real problem is our failure to listen to *ourselves*. We fail in this regard when we look outwardly and comparatively to define 'self'. And, in the process, we lose 'self'. In truth, we must first be driven inward (to our very souls) before we can subsequently look outwardly to others. Must look into our own hearts *before* we can share those hearts with others toward the greater good.

In the Biblical 1st Testament story of Adam and Eve, we're taught that the two first human beings of this world laid the initial seed of inherited sinfulness for all subsequent generations. Because they sinned against God. But the real lesson of their story may not be sin at all. Instead, it's about *from whom* they tried to draw their identity. Adam and Eve wanted to be God. To be like God. To know as God knows. They looked outwardly *before* they looked inwardly. What if they had done the opposite? You know, first looked into their own hearts instead of coveting what someone else had? We can all learn from this story. For we all need to be 'of' God, not 'like' God.

If we live our lives far more 'of' God and listen to the voice already in us, we'll *also* listen to our own DNA. Those genes will guide us to think whole versus 'what's mine' far more often in our lives. Real kindness. Not a trickle-down kind of kindness. Not leaving the leftovers or the residual, collateral benefits of our individual wealth and prosperity to others. Rather, we'll give of the 'first fruits' of our labor and toil. Guided by the real *Invisible Hand*. Not our hand. But the hand of God. The real and only hand that we need in our quest for identity.

There's No Place Like Home

What is our True North, the true ground of our identity? Where are we most centered in our lives right now? Where is our 'home'? For many of us, the answer lies in where we reside. The physical structures of our houses, our apartments, our condos, or our school dormitories. Or even more broadly, our hometowns. For others, home is characterized by our place of worship: our church, synagogue, mosque, or temple. Or a sacred city, shrine, statue, or retreat. For yet others, it's their 'happy place'—their escape or their destination of choice. In these instances, home has geographic or structural roots and meaning.

Conversely, in the corporate world, the notion of 'home' is more commercial. It's how companies build loyalty and grounding toward the company and its products. As consumers, we begin to consciously or unconsciously identify with a product's feel, packaging, cost, quality, reputation, or value. When we walk down the aisles of a store, we actively seek out the product as a result. For it's become a 'home', of sorts, for meeting our human needs, however manipulated we've become in the process.

While home is often physical, geographical, or commercial, it's also emotional. Perhaps nothing describes this better than the iconic movie, *The Wizard of Oz*. Who can forget Dorothy's famous line towards the end of the film? She said, "If I ever go looking for my heart's desire again, I won't look any further than my own back yard. Because if it isn't there, I never really lost it to begin with." With those words, she tapped her heels and repeated the phrase, "There's no place like home." And she was magically transported home. For Dorothy and for many of us, home is about feelings. Deep feelings linked inextricably with memories of family, love, food, holidays, celebrations, and milestones. Our hearts ground us squarely there. There's no place like home.

But what if home's greatest meaning isn't about our feelings? Not about a location or a destination. Not a matter of something external to us. Perhaps not even about our hearts, if by so saying we mean our emotional attachments. Rather, what if our truest home is our True North? Our integrity as individual persons. More importantly, the *Intentional Integrity of our respective identities*. Because when we're integrity-based inside, we're joined-up with ourselves. We're clear about who we really are. What we stand for. Our meaning, purpose, values, and vision for our lives. We're firmly grounded, aligned, and integrated around these things. Centered. Authentic. Consistent. Both feet planted firmly.

To be sure, many things impede this notion of home for us. Our 'big picture' is often obscured by the pressures of daily living. Perhaps we're victims of poor role modeling in our lives. We've been taught the false virtues of simply getting along. Going along. Taking the wide path. Following the crowd. Staying in the slow lane. Poor boundaries don't help, either. Setbacks and losses can keep us on our back feet, as well. The work of healing can feel like a full-time job. And it can set us on new paths, not always in alignment with our real sense of self and our truest identity.

Here's a thought, though. What if the greatest block to our integrity lies not outside of us? Not external to us. But from within. For intentional integrity requires our human will. Finding our truest spiritual home, this place of our grounding and identity in integrity, is a choice. And not just a choice, but also a discipline. A lifetime of repetition and practice. It starts with this core question: what do I want to 'be' about in my life? What is my brand—my core principles and values? What about me should transcend the pressures and whims of today? And become my legacy for tomorrow. For all times, even after I'm gone.

Then, once grounded in who I want to be, I need to choose the actions that best align with my vision of integrity. Not just choose, but also choose wisely. Because actions are not all created equally, as they say. I need to cast a 'critical', discerning eye on the specific things that actually move me toward my vision. What actions propel integrity in my life and in my being? And why? How? It's important that I get clear and adjust accordingly. Conversely, which actions hinder my progress and blur my true identity? Why and how? Further, when I've identified these 'blockers', I must have the intestinal fortitude to change. To stop the things that get in the way. The things that cloud the clarity around what I want to be at my very core. It's certainly not easy. In truth, it's a challenging quest that never ends.

While actions matter greatly, they must be actually built on a *foundation* of honesty. About myself. Now being honest with myself doesn't mean condemning myself. It doesn't mean my self-rejection, deprecation, or a centering hatred. But it *does* require my curiosity. An openness to see myself realistically as I should. A willingness to hold an unbiased mirror to my face and to my heart. The courage to remain curious and open to change. Like so many things in the spiritual life, holding a mirror to myself requires that I question my heart. Integrity demands a spirit of honest inquiry. And the discernment to distinguish between my *intentions versus my intentionality*.

In getting to the root of this intention/intentionality distinction, it's important to explore the following: how is what I believe different than what I do? How is what I think different than what I do? The same for what I value. What I want to achieve in my life. And what I want to enjoy in my life. If I'm well aligned, then great! I should keep at it. But if they're different, I have a connectivity problem. A disjointed integrity. Having said that, here's the beauty of human life as gifted to me by God: I'm free to live and to 'be' more fully. To change. To continuously grow and better flourish in my identity. To become more intentionally integrated.

Lasting change thus begins with a choice. With big dreams. With honest and sometimes difficult questions. With reflection and discernment. With small or big steps. With actions. And with daily discipline and practice. But it's possible. For me. For everyone. Possible if we're brave and resolute. If we're determined to live our own lives, not someone else's. Determined to set and keep the goals necessary to be our truest selves more fully and integrally. To stay focused on the prize. And, in so doing, to say 'yes' far more often to the most important, not urgent, things in our lives. Conversely, to say 'no' far more often to those things which merely get in the way. No matter how enticing or tempting they may seem in the moment.

Like Dorothy in the *Wizard of Oz*, we can click our own heals and can be transported. Not to return to our back yard in Kansas. Nor to travel to another place or time or space. But, instead, to find our own 'True North'. Our own identity of *Intentional Integrity*. It's an inside job. It's about what's inside of us. About our very 'being'. For there's no place like home.

The Gift of Light Within

As spiritual people of belief and faith, it's easy to feel that we're called to help others in need. To come alongside those who are poor, mournful, meek, seeking peace, and persecuted. To shine a light on justice, peace, comfort, support, and mercy for them. To help them out. To show them the way. But this might miss the point completely. For what if the very people whom we try to help *already* have the qualities of spiritual identity that God is seeking? These qualities are already in them. In fact, Jesus was asking us to become far more like these folks. Like the meek and humble and poor and persons of peace. Because these are the very things that matter in the end. The things that make us human beings in God's image and likeness.

In my past work as a chaplain, I was often asked to pray for patients and their families. To do so in the midst of life's most terrible trials, sickness, loss and sorrow, suffering, pain, hopelessness and sadness, and fear. I was asked for words of comfort, encouragement, wisdom, praise, and insight. And, while I typically spent far more time listening than speaking, I did offer such prayers and words along the way at appropriate times.

But I also learned this: the greatest words, prayers, gifts, insights, sources of inspiration, and thanks never came from me. Nor from the mouths of other chaplains or pastors or priests. For, however hard we tried, the power of truest identity came most often from within the very hearts of those who suffered. A power fueled by God and by their own spirituality. Visited by the Spirit, perhaps. Harnessed by whatever source of transcendence that they found meaningful. But coming from within themselves, nonetheless.

The greatest prayer that I ever heard came not from my mouth. Instead, it was from a patient in a hospital where I served. The patient prayed in simple, direct terms. It was almost childlike. Pure. Thoughtful. Innocent. Thankful. Trusting. It was simply beautiful. Following the patient's prayer, she asked me to pray. I did, but I felt very small in doing so. I told the patient that whatever I might now say paled in comparison to the sheer might, splendor, and wisdom of her own previous words. And then I feebly spoke to God. I reminded God that God had just heard the wisest, most incredible words that I may have ever heard. I asked God to truly hear her. Why would I want to spoil her words to God with mine?

The greatest wisdom that I ever heard was not from teachers or professors or doctors or nurses or social workers or even other chaplains. I learned far more from the patients themselves. I visited one patient who told me that his own pit of suffering was one that he'd built himself. He had laid the foundations and the walls of this suffering. He became lost because he stopped trying to find a way *within* it all.

In this regard, the patient told me that it was only in getting older, in facing his own pending mortality, that he could truly find the gift of knowing what was most important in the end. That it was only by embracing the vast mysteries of God, and the many questions posed by these mysteries, that he could ever find ultimate truth. The patient told me it was only by his becoming a burden to others that he could see the importance of carrying the burdens of others each day. That only in letting go of things could he truly acquire the things that he needed most at this time in his life. Finally, that it was only in his sorrows, losses, and limitations that he was now able to know true freedom, joy, and laughter.

The greatest gift that I ever received as a chaplain wasn't a plaque. Not a certificate. Not a book. Not a good review. Not a paycheck. Not even close. The greatest gift was a hug from grieving families as I later left the hospital room of their now-passed relatives. A gift of thanks for coming. For sitting with them. For simply being there. For sometimes offering words of comfort, Scripture, and prayer. But mostly for taking the time to care. What a gift. And from people who somehow found a way to say 'thank you' on the worst day of their lives.

The greatest gesture of appreciation that I ever received was from a homeless patient who was leaving the hospital after an extended stay. We had spent a number of visits together. The patient's face outwardly beamed as she prepared to depart. She could hardly contain her smile. She turned to me and said, "Thank you for everything, chaplain. I won't forget." And as she spoke, she turned to leave. Everything that she owned was packed tightly onto a baby stroller that she wheeled from the hospital. This was her home on the streets. And I felt valued in a profound, nearly indescribable way that day. Humbled by the resilient spirit of another human being.

The greatest things that I ever received in my pastoral work came from the hearts of the patients, themselves. I have looked into the blank, numbed faces of those who were physically or emotionally abused as children or as adults. I have looked into the wounded hearts of those who grew up amidst drug and alcohol addiction in their families of origin. I have searched the hearts of those who lost their soul fighting bloody wars in foreign lands. I have sat with those who lost their children, parents, family, and friends in cases of sudden, traumatic deaths. I have shared the concurrent joy, sorrow, memories, grief, and confusion as family members stood bedside with a dying loved one when aggressive life support was being withdrawn.

I have held the promise of my accompaniment and hope to those who find no reason to go on or to live another day. I have befriended those whose only present and reliable friend was a bottle of vodka. I have listened to those with only days to live as they came to terms with their fears, hopes, legacies, losses, regrets, and their proudest moments. I have tried to hear those who suffer. To listen very intently. Not just to their stories and their words, but to their feelings, their affects, and to their very souls. Those things may be unspoken, but are deeply moving within them.

The truest beauty, the truest answers, the truest insights, and the truest gifts belong to those who suffer. They come not from bookshelves or the countless stacks in a seminary library. They do not come from the pulpit at church. They don't come from a lectern in a lecture hall. Not from a journal. Not from the sage wisdom of a noted philosopher. Not from those wearing a collar or the sacred garments of a priest or pastor.

No. They come from those who wear faded patient hospital gowns. From those who live on the streets. Who face sudden or chronic illnesses. Who are struggling through the 'sunset years' of their lives. And who now face their own mortality. Who have lost all power to control things anymore. Who see their very finiteness and limits in stark, real, and darkly vivid terms. Who have every reason to give up, to pull away, to close down, to shut out, or to close out.

But they do not. These courageous people have faced their suffering. They have looked this suffering squarely in the eye. And they didn't blink. Because they took the quest for their truest identities and decided to let God in. To let God work in it, not outside of it. To let God ruminate within their bodies and within their souls. To let God be God. To let God draw nearer in the process. And, in turn, to restore their souls. Their very God-given, innate capacity and responsibility for Spiritual fullness and integration as unconditionally loved human 'beings'. This is their gift. Their profound gift within. Their profound gift to us.

'Quest'-ions for Prayer and Further Reflection

- In what ways are your own spirituality and identity being co-opted, to your detriment, by institutions, practices, or entrenched and rigid belief systems?

- Is your locus of control largely external? If so, how and why are you allowing outside circumstances, random chance, or other persons to rule your life?

- How are your beliefs, feelings, and actions consciously or unconsciously influenced by your own negative assumptions, fears, unspoken wants and needs, past experiences, or untold stories?

- How could you become more spiritually aware of and connected with your identity in God, your purpose, your talents, your relationships, and a more positive, healthy, and integral vision for your life?

- What untapped wisdom, light, love, and direction already reside deeply within you? How can you listen to these internal things more intently and purposefully each day?

Our Quest for Wellbeing

Wellbeing:

- *A state of feeling comfortable and stable*
- *The relative absence of anxiety and fear*
- *Achieving equilibrium and security in one's life*
- *Avoidance of risk, danger, hurt, or injury*
- *Maintaining personal contentment and happiness*

The Sacred Path of Non-Violence

Tick. Tick. Tick. Man down. Woman down. Now another. And another. Time is running. People fleeing. Quickly fleeing. Don't delay. Get out of here. Shots fired. "Everyone down. Now. To the floor. Take cover. Take shelter. Run." Insufficient provocation. Overzealous prosecution. Not in self-defense. Ambush in retaliation. Countless injured. Random violence. Violent crime. Soldiers. Cops. Line of duty. Won't come home now. Towns are mourning. Civil wars and bombed-out buildings. Body counts and children wailing. On our streets. In public places. In our homes, domestic violence. People screaming. People sobbing. People shouting. Loss of feeling. Keep alert. Be vigilant. Soft target. Hard target. Concealed weapon. Look out. "It's the world we live in. Don't give in. Live your lives. Get on with it." That's what they say. So we get numb. It's the way it is, I guess. Surrender.

But Tick. Tick. Tick. Time is running. Out on us. Because we're 'outing' us. It's the Next Extinction. Not a drought. Not a famine. Not a meteor strike. No, it's our strike on us. Our killing fields. Not-so-friendly fire. Not in the least. We're in the crossfire. Our own to be exact. To the bitter end. Our end, to be clear. What possesses us? To hurt and wound? To kill another? To take a life? The one now gone was a father, too. A mother. Child. Sister. Friend. But gone too soon. Only tears and grief remain. Another soul now lost to us. And the tears we shed are not just ours. They're God's as well. God cries too. With anguish. At a light snuffed out. A soul bled out. A life gone out. So when is enough, enough? How many more senseless deaths are too many? Before we Stand-Down. And put our weapons down. Put our hate down. Anger too. Sit down. Bow down. Calm down. Dial it down. And stop talking down to others.

And cherish each life. For they all matter. Because they are of God. From God. We are meant to hold, not to hurt. We are meant to heal and help, not to harm. We are meant to love, not to hate. We are meant to stand up, not to fall. If only we'll first Stand-Down. In Peace. Friendship. Just Communion. Reconciliation. We have a choice. No one will do it for us. It's ours to do. For ourselves. For each other. For the sake of sacred life. For our family's sake. For the world's sake. For God's sake. There has to be a better way to solve our problems. A way of peace. A way of wellbeing. What if we chose to Stand-Down? One person at a time. Just in time. It's time.

Jail Break

In the wake of the continued onslaught of violent shootings around the world, we continuously hear the ongoing lament, 'We're at the crossroads', as we struggle to contain an increasingly violent global society. Sadly, we left the crossroads some time ago. We have passed the tipping point, and are rapidly descending into the abyss of chaos when it comes to respect for human life, safety, and shared wellbeing.

Well-meaning voices are sounding the alarm that things are different now. For the number, frequency, magnitude, and sheer brutality of our violent acts against each other are unparalleled in history. This is true, but people have been dying every day in towns and cities throughout our world for a long time due to acts of senseless violence. Mass killings certainly represent an unspeakable new low, but we have been steadily arriving here for decades.

We rightly pray for and comfort the families and communities of the victims. We should do no less. There will certainly be continued calls for greater gun control, especially in the United States—a place where many see individual gun ownership rights as untouchable and nearly 'sacred'.

However, you can count on this: we cannot depend on our governments to get this epidemic of violence under control. Nor can we retreat to the false comfort of innocuous statements such as, "Guns don't kill people. People kill people."

In truth, people kill people with many instruments. But terrifyingly more potent weaponry makes this killing much easier and more horrific. The world, especially the United States, cries out for an adult discussion around gun violence. However, the real conversation must go far deeper. It must reach into our very souls as a people of peace and good will. It requires collective reflection and decisions. But it starts with each one of us individually. And it begins with this question: when will we awaken to the false reality of a freedom and 'safety' grounded in fear– grounded in our capacity for wanton, random destruction? Have all our guns made us any safer?

Ask the countless families scarred forever by violent crimes and terrorism. Are we any freer or safer when we have to lock ourselves tightly in our homes? Is life well lived when our children cannot attend school or walk in their neighborhoods without fear of violence? Are we any more connected to each other in community when our heads are buried in TV, movie, and gaming violence that teaches us to hate and disrespect each other? Are we truly 'whole' human beings when our life's purpose has degenerated into immediate gratification seeking, requiring no vision for a better future ... beyond our own self-interest or narrow definitions of self-defense and 'safety' against the acts of others?

The only surprise here is that we are surprised at all with the outcomes. And the 'patient' is now on life-support. In truth, we're sick patients set adrift from hope in a violent, unsafe, and flat-lining world. We are failing. But looking to someone else to solve this for us is a ruse. That constitutes weakness and dependency. Now we surely need stricter, more definitive gun policies and laws. But the real answer lies *within us*. I challenge our nation and our world, one person at a time, to voluntarily lay down our weapons. Do the counterintuitive thing. Let us show what real courage is. Real courage is choosing to live a life firmly grounded in peace. We will all be safer in the long run, and we will have done it in the spirit of freedom and shared wellbeing.

It's also time to voluntarily lay down our violent video games and other misdirected 'entertainment'. Time to make a statement for spending 'caring' time with each other —not with our machines. Further, it's time to turn off our smart phones far more often and look around. We need to look for and look after those who could use our protection, help, conversation, or simply a loving smile. It is time to think about a life dedicated to making a positive difference, not about our preserving some individualized and misguided sense of our 'rights' in keeping us artificially safe and comfortable. It is time to turn toward others in love.

The nation of the United States was founded on individual liberty. But we'll only be a free nation once again if we soberly admit that we're currently imprisoned on death row. We'll only be free when we acknowledge that real power comes not from our will, but from our hearts. We will only become human again when we say 'No' to life as it is now defined for us. That kind of life is, in reality, not one of safety or wellbeing. It's one of individualized, selfish death. For we were made by God to love each other in community. Admittedly, living life in this way is risky. We could feel alone and 'unsafe' in the beginning. But others will follow our lead and our example. And we cannot give up. We must make a commitment for the long run for a change.

Please join in a battle worth fighting. Please join in refusing to give into the inevitable alienation and further senseless death that surely lies ahead of us. Join in truly honoring the lives of those lost to violence. Join in recapturing the fullness of our humanity and the greatness of a people who make a positive and lasting difference. The 'arms' that I call you to are not guns or knives or even smart phones. They are the loving, outstretched arms of people who welcome each other in God's name and grace — in an enormously worthwhile cause of a true life of wellbeing together.

False Promises

There's a technique called 'bait and switch' when you're buying something. It happens when the seller entices you into the purchase with a shiny, glitzy, brand spanking-new product. Only to then substitute it with something far less glamorous or less feature-functional after you've handed over your money to the merchant. In other words, you don't get what you've actually paid for. The only real antidote for this trap is to follow the 'buyer beware' principle when shopping. Check out everything carefully before you pay for anything.

What if we now extended this idea more broadly to living in general? In what ways are our mad dash for wellbeing akin to 'bait and switch'? We're

Our Quest for Wellbeing

sold a bill of goods when all we really want is a little peace. Elusive and frustrating indeed. In this regard, countless thousands of people are drawn to the United States of America each year as immigrants. New entrants may seek safety or refuge from brutal regimes, warfare, and violence. At other times, they seek high skill positions in real need here. But often, immigrants really seek the 'American Dream'. This dream is different and personal for each newcomer. But it typically entails notions of greater freedom, opportunity, advancement, quality of life, technology, infrastructural amenities, personal safety, and wellbeing. On the flip side, current citizens already living here chase wellbeing through getting ahead, greater affluence, possession of things, discretionary money to spend, and the latest technology.

All well and good to be sure. But do those things make any of us happier or even safer in our own 'beings'? The United Nations publishes an annual Happiness Index, which is based on questions posed to a sampling of respondents in a variety of countries. The United States is certainly not last on the happiness list. Our general affluence overall and a decent supporting societal infrastructure ensure that we aren't near the bottom. But we're also not at the top of the list either. What contributes to our lagging relative performance?

Increasing income inequality, mistrust of institutions, a sense of isolation and fear, and a fracturing of community all contribute to our lower than average placement on the Index. According to some, we're also stressed out, tired out, washed out, and left out. We can't relax. We can't enjoy the simple things in life. And we've forgotten that shared time with family and friends matters most of all in our lives. We're anything but safely and snuggly comfortable 'in our own skin'. Many of us are rarely content. Perhaps fewer still feel wellbeing in their souls.

Now it's easy to blame any number of things on our relative lack of felt wellbeing and inner peace. These days, some blame technology, specifically the idea that we all have our 'heads in it'. All the time, in fact. And our heads are always down. Staring blankly into our phones or our tablets. As a result, we've lost our former ability to relate to each other on a truly human level. We'd rather tweet or text or post a picture or a video. In other cases, we blame our relentless rat race to get ahead. To acquire wealth. To buy and use 'stuff'. Worse yet, we've become addicted to all this stuff, and we need to better compartmentalize it in our lives.

To be sure, these and many other things exacerbate our lack of felt joyfulness and wellbeing as people. But they're not really the underlying problems at all. Rather, they're visible symptoms of a deeper problem within us. To be fair, things like human advancement, money, and technology have wonderful and positive potential. When used properly, they can help to solve problems, heal and cure medical illnesses, extend our human life expectancy, lift millions out of poverty, foster exploration, advance the sciences, break down barriers in our increasingly global society, and foster greater safety. But they are *not* the answer to our happiness. Thinking so is 'buying' false promises.

Better regulating our consumption-driven desires (keeping them in-check) won't do the trick here, either. For trying to compartmentalize them entirely misses the point. Because the point is that these things aren't the point at all. They aren't an end-point in our human equation of wellbeing. Instead, they're simply tools in our toolkit for living. To be used as needed. With great discretion and wisdom. For when you're a hammer (and only a hammer), *everything* looks like a nail. A nail that needs a good pounding. We've been doing a pretty good job of pounding each other and ourselves, to be honest. With a blunt instrument. Based on false promises.

The great 20th Century American playwright and novelist Thornton Wilder said this about money: "The difference between a little money and no money at all is enormous—and can shatter the world. And the difference between a little money and an enormous amount of money is very slight—and that, also, can shatter the world." Wilder said this in the context of Wilder's other quote about money. He characterized money as being like manure—because it needs to be spread around. At this point, you're probably wondering what this quote possibly has to do with wellbeing. For Wilder was talking about money in the narrow sense of the word. You'd be right in one sense. But, given the kind of man Wilder was, perhaps he had a wider meaning in mind.

In the most basic sense, Wilder argued that human beings are severely hampered by an inability to provide the basic financial necessities of life. Conversely, the ability to more affirmatively provide for these necessities across society creates greater balance and general wellbeing. Having said that, though, chasing after ever-greater accumulations of individual wealth and possessions beyond the level of meeting necessities results in increasingly diminishing returns relative to its detrimental effects on others.

But what if we took Wilder's ideas even further yet? And applied them more specifically to spiritual 'wellbeing'? In this regard, the difference between a little wellbeing and none at all is enormous. And it can shatter the world . . . as well as shatter us. For when we feel a deep, abiding, internal wellbeing void, we try to fill it. Very often with external stuff like chasing the 'dream', getting ahead, making a lot of money, and drowning in technology. Sadly enough, these things are quite willing and eager to enter into and fill the empty spaces within us.

What's worse, though, is that they begin to define us as individuals. For we internalize this stuff in ways that the stuff actually *becomes* our embodiment. And it can quickly crowd out anything of greater spiritual meaning and identity. If so, why in the world do we do it? Some of us internalize external things because we don't like the feeling of being void. Or we may simply not like ourselves in the first place. Or we buy the lies and false promises of the 'bait and switch' artists of the world. Filling our souls with this stuff may feel comfortable, safe, and more certain. Tangible. A quick fix. But in the process, we've now commoditized ourselves. Allowed something external to ourselves define us. And, in the process, we've wittingly or unwittingly de-constructed our very souls and beings.

So we've seen that investing *something* in our wellbeing truly matters. Failing to do so saps our very spiritual lifeblood from us as we get co-opted by externalities. Given that, let's take the Wilder's quote analogy to human wellbeing to its second part. The difference between a little wellbeing and an enormous amount is slight. But its impact can be significant and life changing. For once we've invested in building up our wellbeing to some small degree, we're already well on the way.

Each small, incremental improvement from there makes a big difference. It makes a difference even if the progress outwardly appears to be slow. Even if well-meaning people in our lives start questioning the changes in us. Even if they're encouraging us to resume living the false promises that they have long settled into. Small steps forward result in unalterable momentum and continuous progress if we stay at the process with some discipline.

A number of things can help us in this regard. We can set greater boundaries upfront about the things that get in the way of our true wellbeing. Realistically speaking, we've already acknowledged that the absence of sufficient money, a vocation, future plans for advancement, adequate technology, and other things can constitute huge 'dissatisfy-ers' in our lives. But we must *also* remember that the presence of them is rarely, if ever, a lasting satisfier. Instead, we can establish our lives on other things: ideals like gratitude, contentment, trust, centeredness and balance, impermanence, empowerment, and transcendent meaning, to name a few. Further, we can live with a greater sense of embodied grace and generosity. Not just towards others, but also towards us.

Next, we can endeavor to more intentionally live less anxiously each day. Fear and anxiety are crippling our lives. When we're frightened in a generalized way, we constrict ourselves. We pull back. We become more vigilant and less curious. We get less trusting of ourselves and of others. And we become less hopeful and more protective. Conversely, when we live less anxiously, we more actively pursue internal joyfulness, not fulfillment. For fulfillment presumes that we need to regularly refill ourselves with things external to us. A better way is to seek internal joy. Joyfulness that transcends momentary happiness or a sense that we're artificially fulfilled.

Perhaps the greatest key in all of this, though, is seemingly paradoxical. We need to quit trying to *find* wellbeing as individual seekers on the quest. Because when we work to 'find' something, it also implies that the found thing can be possessed, held onto, or achieved. But it's a false promise. That's because our wellbeing isn't something that we find or achieve in the end. Rather, it emerges from within us as we strive to live differently each day. By seeking 'who' we really are in God, in our communities, and in the world.

In so doing, we can organically *discover* our inherent capacity for greater wellbeing. While also *uncovering* (and finally discarding) the false promises that have far-too-often guided us in the past. The false promises that can never really satisfy us at a spiritual level. For these promises are illusionary and temporal. They may temporarily relieve our existential pain. But the absence of pain is *not* true wellbeing. It's not 'being' at all, really. And the absence of feeling or being is simply nothing. So . . . 'Buyer Beware'. And choose something else for a change.

Step Out of Line

We wait in lines for nearly everything in life. To pay for groceries. To buy movie tickets. To enter theaters for a show or for a concert. Or stadiums for a ball game. And, invariably, someone's always in front of us in line. Perhaps they got there earlier than we did. Conversely, someone's usually behind us in the line, as well. They arrived later than we did and are now further back. But, short of people cutting into the line, we're all in the line together. Arriving earlier means being further forward. Arriving later means standing further back. Fairly simple. Generally fair. We're all equals of sorts in the line.

Now when I'm waiting in a line, I see mostly the backs of people in front of me. Not their faces usually. Unless, of course, they happen to turn around. And I can't really hear them either. For their faces and their mouths are turned away from me. I can't, therefore, ever really know them as 'persons'. Even if we end up talking together for a minute or two, it's mostly about superficial topics. Surface level. Small talk. Like when we talk about the weather. Or why they're here today. Nothing of any real substance. Awareness stuff only. Maybe that's better than not knowing anything about them, I guess. For no harm is done. We spent some light 'surface-level time' together while we all stood in line.

In my past work as a chaplain, I have spent lots of time with people. But it was rarely surface-level time. We didn't talk much about the weather or last night's game. Or about current affairs in the world, to be honest. Instead, we talked about far deeper things. Existential stuff. Using profound words. Most often, the words came from the mouths of those suffering physically, medically, and emotionally. In some cases from those who were also suffering marginalization as people. The 'non-persons' of the world. You know, the ones that we've pushed to the back of the line. Not because they arrived late. But because we don't see them as enough 'like us'.

And, given that they're not 'like us', we've placed them in the back on purpose. They can't seem to step out of the line, no matter how hard they try to move. For accepted notions of empowerment feel quite illusionary. Empowerment is faintly there and is possible, I suppose. But it's always distant. Always close enough to stretch and reach for, but usually just beyond one's grasp. It's a cruel reality. Like the 'carrot and the stick' technique, but with the carrot enticingly dangled—then suddenly and violently yanked away.

In many ways, it's audacious and presumptuous for me to speak on behalf of the poor, the elderly, women, people of color, the homeless, scarred veterans of war, the chronically sick, or the LGBTQ community. I don't fit within any of these. I happen to sit in the white male category. I was born into a degree of white privilege. I've never felt rejected on account of being perceived as less worthy or 'on the margins of the acceptable'. I can't recall ever worrying about where my next meal was coming from . . . or where I'd sleep tonight. Therefore, I have no right to pretend that I even remotely understand their plights. But I'm going to share a little of what I've humbly learned from some people in my past pastoral work.

We often use the word 'empowerment' in the sense of our taking control of our lives and our emotions. As another way of saying that we 'need to move on'. We have to 'get over it'. We must somehow 'get past it' or 'put it away'. We're all empowered to move on, I suppose. But, for people we've marginalized, there are few good actual expressions of it. Some exercise 'empowerment' by no longer participating. By simply quitting and walking away. Others remain, but hide their true feelings about what's aggrieved them. Some lie about themselves to feel better or more important. Still others artificially create safety by 'wearing a mask'. You know, creating a pseudo-self of sorts.

The very notion of moving on in any way, however dysfunctional, can feel impossible. Because the persons that we've relegated to the back of the line are often trapped. In many cases, we've created or reduced their choices in the 'game of life'. You know, the game that's typically played within the narrow lines already drawn by those in charge. In this game, exercising 'empowerment' by flight or non-participation only singles oneself out as avoidant or afraid. Speaking up against the system is perceived as combative and resistant. Judgments are made . . . by those with the power and authority to decide. Given this, what does empowered moving on really amount to? Does choice really exist? The sad truth is there isn't any in many cases. Let's take a closer look.

Economically poor and otherwise marginalized children don't choose to be born poor. They don't choose to face deprivations and derision growing up. Children of poor immigrants to the U.S. don't choose to speak a 'foreign' language as their primary one, while their school friends speak only English. They don't choose to be seen as outsiders. Impoverished children don't choose to be dependent on outsiders for financial support, despite their parents working multiple jobs. These children don't choose any of it. They don't feel empowered. They don't feel safe. This certainly isn't wellbeing.

Persons of color don't choose to be discriminated against on the basis of their color or ethnicity. The chronically ill and dependent don't choose to become a burden on others. Persons of the Muslim faith don't choose to be spuriously profiled and stereotyped as 'extreme Islamic terrorists', despite the fact that they live their daily lives with dignity in our country—working hard, contributing to our communities, and extending love to others.

Women don't choose to be cast as second-class citizens, earning less than their male counterparts for the same work. Female employees don't choose misogynistic male bosses who somehow see all non-male staff members as playthings, not people.

In these instances, and many more, people don't feel empowered. Why should they, for that matter? But this is much, much deeper than simply empowerment actually. The pain is literally an *existential* and spiritual one for many marginalized people. Like the loss of a dear, loved family member or a longtime friend. The hole in their heart does not go away. They don't ever really get over it. The hole is never really filled. It's a permanent loss. Of a part of them.

It's the hole of a childhood lost. Of a life torn away. Of a sense of being and feeling different and devalued. Of needing to take the handouts of others, no matter how 'small' this makes them feel. Of never feeling settled in their heart. Of being afraid, abused, and taken advantage of. Of not being wanted at all, really. No one ever gets over that. For it's a part of their very personhood. They move on with their lives and their work in spite of it. They manage the existential hole. They don't fill it with something else. And they try to resist others trying to fill it with cement.

Talking about their past can help. It helps when others join them in their stories in a spirit of love and respect. And deeply listen at multiple levels. To their words, their feelings, their affects, their hearts, and their souls. Those pushed to the back of the line don't seek pity from others. Instead, they seek persons who are willing to come alongside them in witness and mutual support. What they don't need is careless, superficial talk. Or dumb statements, dumb generalizations, or dumb questions, however well intended.

In this process of listening to and trying to support another, there's an important saying: never kick the props out from under someone unless you're prepared to replace these props with something better. Alternatively, never pull off a scab unless you have a Band-Aid and ointment at the ready. For when you just superficially join someone with well-meaning but unhelpful advice, it's like buzzing the tower in a fighter jet. It makes a lot of noise and rattles everything. But it's destructive and it's reckless. Even when it's accompanied by a measure of positive intent, it only serves to kick the props out from under others. It simply pulls their scabs off. Then it walks away from them and lets them 'bleed out'. And all they see is your back. As *they* take yet one more step further back in the line. While you stay in place or take another step forward without them.

For when we listen superficially, advise negligently, and walk away from those at the back, we've disrespected them, however unconsciously. We've demonstrated a felt sense of superiority over them, even if we don't outwardly want to do so. We may simply feel pity. You know, feel sorry for them. But they neither need nor want any of these things. They've already experienced enough of them growing up or living in their disempowered environments. They don't want to be 'victims' either. They don't like the look of it in themselves or in others. As such, their only real option is to 'get over it' . . . once again. At the back of the line. While the holes in their hearts grow a bit larger and deeper.

If we're to truly join those in line, we need to come alongside them far more fully. And stay there. We need to sit with their stories and be witnesses to them. To join them in mutually empowering ways. To do so no matter how difficult, unsafe, and awkward it feels for you. And to do so together. Not in a line. But by *Stepping Out of Line into a Circle*. Face to face. Heart to heart. Spiritual soul to spiritual soul. If we do so, there's finally some real hope. There's a start.

If we don't, however . . . if we demand that everyone stays in their respective places in line . . . the disempowered know their only 'live' option: they can, once-again, move on, get over it, and put it all behind them. They can, once-again, cover up their wounds with frayed, oft used tissue paper. They can, once again, endeavor to rebuild their 'safety' props using the existing tools in their toolbox. And, of course, they'll have to do so according to the 'keep in line' instructions provided by someone else. But that's not really empowerment, though. They already know this. Because they've learned and lived it existentially at the back of the line while standing firmly disempowered by others.

Powerful Near-Sightedness

Superman is one of our most enduring superheroes. He presents a model of power, reflecting our pervasive, current thinking in many ways. Which one of us has not, at one time or another, associated ourselves with the power and might of Superman—used in the service of truth, justice, and the American Way? Superman embodies a strength that transcends our normal human condition. He bends steel with his bare hands. He leaps tall buildings in a single bound, and speedily travels through air and space. He sees through walls with his X-Ray vision. He is always there to the rescue, just in time. Always doing the right thing with his power, dealing decisively with evil and villainous forces. He never seems to change. While *we* age and face life's increasing infirmities, Superman retains his looks and his strength. He is ostensibly the perfect model of power.

How ironic, then, that Superman's origins were, in fact, not on the planet Krypton. Instead, his genesis was in the highly creative minds of two poor Depression-Era kids from inner city Cleveland. Jerry Siegel and Joe Shuster were unassuming and hardly noteworthy students. They weren't heralded athletes in their school. Nor were they the school presidents. Probably not voted by their peers as 'most likely to succeed' either. They were, instead, two aspiring young men from poor families.

They created the Superman character on the back of torn wallpaper and paper bags while huddled, shivering in their unheated apartments. One of the two suffered near-sightedness and wore glasses in order to see. Frustrated by the initial brush-back from comic syndicates, the two eventually sold their rights to Superman for a pittance, and spent the rest of their lives trying to recover even a fraction of the royalties and profits that spun off from America's subsequent fascination with the Superman story. They lived their lives in unjust obscurity, overrun by powers far greater than themselves. If only Superman had come to their rescue to make things right.

In the same way that Superman concentrates power in his mighty hands, too much power continues to reside in the hands of a relatively few in our world today. This power is often individualized and motivated by selfish interests, versus being vested in our communities for the welfare of the whole. Too many people remain outside the sphere of power as we currently define it. Too many also lack the opportunity to act as positive agents in their own lives. Too much power remains out of alignment with God's plan for its rightful use. One need not look too hard or too long at many of our streets and communities to notice.

If we look closely, we don't see God's vision of power, but a *distortion* of God's power. And we don't need even remotely perfect vision to do so. When we see a homeless family huddling beneath a cardboard shelter in the rain, we see a distortion of power. When we witness paternalistic and condescending behaviors toward those we consider our 'inferiors' in this world, we see a distortion of power. When we neglect the human needs right before our very eyes, we see a distortion of power. When we visualize powerlessness manifested through hopelessness and malaise, substance abuse and addiction, domestic violence, marginalization of others, and poverty, we see a distortion of power.

Fortunately, the distortion of power will not have the final word. We do not require the 'just in time' rescue by Superman. Instead, we require the 'for all time' rescue by our real Superhero, God. God's message of rescue is very simple: accept me, accept my love, and follow my way forward. God's way entails not a distortion of power, but God's intended use of power. God's way defines power as emanating from God, not from ourselves or from the few who now appear to hold power in our world today. God's plan redefines power in a truly relational and communal way—fostering economic and social justice, dignity, hospitality toward others, empowerment, and respect for all. A power that plants the seeds of God's hope and God's hope for us all. We *all* have an active role to play in this. It involves not merely throwing money at it from a safe distance. Instead, it requires our getting actively invested and involved.

Unlike the story of Superman, real power is not about some narrow definition of 'Truth, Justice, and the American Way'. It is about God's enduring truth, justice, and way. As such, we need to truly come together under God's 'Cape'. We don't have perfect vision. We can't see through walls with X-Ray vision. We don't need to. In fact, we can do just fine being nearsighted, sometimes squinting to make things out before us. We can put pencil-to-paper using the power that God has given us to draw a different story. With a better ending. One in which we can *all* become 'super' in a different, loving and more caring kind of way. That's powerful 20/20 vision, to be sure.

The Poetry of Chaos

A typical novel or short story's structure can be comforting and reassuring to the reader. It offers constancy and predictability to things when we pick up a book, a magazine, or peruse them from our laptops or tablets. Most stories focus on their respective characters, plots, settings, and the overarching themes. You know, the theme: the thing that we're supposed to figure out from the plot and the characters. The big 'take-away', if you will.

Even the story itself usually progresses in a predictable way. Most often, the author introduces us to the background as we begin the book. It's the author's way of acquainting us with the history, characters, and context for the story. This is typically the slowest part of the 'read', and we're often anxious to speed things up to get to the meat of the story in the pages that follow. And, in fact, that's what usually happens. Next, the author creates a rising action in the plot. We learn about the main problem or conflict in the story. The characters become protagonists. We get hints or a full-frontal hit around the 'good guys' and the 'bad ones'.

Via a slow or speedy 'burn' or build, the author ultimately takes us to the climax of the story, where things reach a crescendo. Periodically with a few twists and turns to keep us a little off-balance. After this, we're gently guided to the story's end through what authors call 'falling action'. Things conclude, however nicely or not, in a resolution. Or as some call it, the 'denouement' of the story. At times, the end is a surprise. At others, it leaves us sad. Sometimes we're even left to guess. Whatever the story's content, though, the basic structure is pretty predictable from story-to-story.

Many of us look at our own lives as this kind of a story. The same goes for the lives of our families. Of our friends. Our co-workers. Even strangers. And we want these 'stories' to have predictability. Life needs to progress in an orderly fashion. Like a book. With a structure. A framework of sorts. And when it no longer does so, we don't like it very much. For painting on a blank canvas is frightening. Even more so when the canvas seems to independently and erratically move around while we're trying to brush our paint on it. In truth, it feels downright chaotic.

Chaos is the opposite of predictability. It's a moving human story without structure. Chaos is what we typically try hardest to avoid. Or battle against. What we regard as existentially 'unsafe' for us. Because it feels like trying to wrestle a greased pig to the ground. Feels like trying to swat at a fly that keeps darting away from us whenever we get close to it on the wall or a window. If we were to give chaos a literary term, we might call it *Poetry*. Most of us had to read poems when we were in school. Many of us had to write a few along the way, as well. Perhaps we gravitated toward 'order' even here, as we tended toward structured lines such as, "Roses are Red, Violets are Blue . . . " For I'd rather have structure, and I'll bet you do too! See . . . it rhymes. Nice orderly flow to it, as well.

But more creative, fluid poetry can teach us something about chaos and change if we're willing to engage with it openly and more spiritually. And drop the "Roses are Red . . . " routine. Poetry can be beautiful chaos, in fact. A bit of literary chaos that can soften our own edges. It can open us to creativity. Get us out of our rut and our need for safety and structure. This is precisely because poetry doesn't need the kind of order that most stories require. Poetry doesn't have to have a genre. We don't have to characterize poems by 'headers' such as fiction and non-fiction. We need not label a poem as a mystery, a thriller, an adventure, a romance, or a sci-fi.

Poems don't need a large cast of characters, either. In fact, they can work just fine with only one: you as writer or you as reader. Actually, poems don't even need complete sentences. They don't have to rhyme, despite your deep, abiding urge to 'force things' in this way. Great poems don't need a plot or a logical sequence or flow to them. Don't require a narrative to follow. For a poem's symbolism can be far more important than any literal meaning that it might spin off in the reading.

This is because the beauty of pure creative imagination or reverie can be far more meaningful than a story line. A poem's expressed fears, hopes, and dreams are often profoundly more critical than any outcomes or resolution that it could ever bring. In short, the relative 'chaos' is one of poetry's best characteristics. It gives a good poem real, unbounded heart and soul. But what does poetry's chaos have to do with our human spirituality and lives? Let's look at some ways that our own experienced chaos parallels a good poem.

For one, life (like a creative, spontaneous poem) can be impulsive. The universe seems to act on its own volition at times. Without logic. Or warning. Or even direction or purpose. In fact, the people around us don't seem to follow the accepted rules at certain points. The natural laws of cause and effect appear to unravel. Things don't follow our commands. Or anyone's for that matter. It feels like logic and reason have been tossed right out the window. Even facts and information are jumbled. Past behaviors and coping mechanisms don't work anymore. It's a total short-circuit. Everything's gone haywire.

If that's not enough, the comforting, soothing inter-dependency of people and things appear to have torn away. We can't seem to negotiate the chaos around us, no matter how hard we try. No matter how good we are at it. Furthermore, the normal reciprocity of things is gone. Everything and everyone looks uncaringly toward us. The world has morphed into an impersonal, autonomous mess. We can even feel like we've lost our place and identity in things. Like a starving poet with a bad case of writer's block, we've become 'author-less'.

Our Quest for Wellbeing

Finally and perhaps most importantly, though, chaos resists our efforts to give some perspective to it. For the seeming chaos in our lives gives us little to hold onto. The very nature of chaotic change makes it nearly impossible to understand or adapt to it. It's brutally difficult to integrate it into our soul. Because it's so diffused and rapidly changing in its own chaotic 'soul'. Somewhat like an improvisational, offbeat, way-out-there poem that makes no sense at all to us.

As challenging as chaos can seem in our lives, though, we can count on it always being there. So, in our respective quests, we must become better 'poets'. It goes without saying that the truest nature of life is the need to live with the many great mysteries of our universe. But how do we do this when we're left with unanswered, difficult questions? As spiritual people of faith, we do so by trusting the Character of God, not judging God for the specific actions that God *seems* to be causing. For God may not be the author of these actions at all. That said, it's possible that God *has* introduced randomness and uncertainty into the universe and our world. But, fortunately, God has also given us something, in love, to deal with it.

We've been given what we most need to 'write poetry' amidst the chaos in our lives: *Capacity*. God has gifted us the capacity to move around in and grow from the chaos. The capacity to truly understand and accept our mortality and our impermanence in the grand scheme of things. The capacity to know that we control very little, actually. That we influence only a little more. We're given the capacity to grasp the important difference between influence and control. We're also gifted with the capacity to let go of that which we can neither control nor influence. To make what sense of things that we can. Then to accept the senselessness of that which we cannot.

It's possible that the greatest gift we have is our capacity to find personal wellbeing *within* the chaos around us. And, like any great poet, to move within the rhythm and motion of the untidiness of it all. To find our way when our maps and our compasses are no longer helpful. To find rest and restoration through contemplation and prayer. And to allow potential 'truths' in multiple, unpredictable, and unplanned narratives in our lives—however seemingly competitive and contradictory on the surface.

Like a good poet, our job is to keep writing in the midst of the chaos. To continue looking for 'openings' in this life. For possibilities. For different narratives, particularly when they make no sense at the moment. That's because the greatest sense of the seemingly senseless is a sense of adventure.

Poetic Adventure. Sometimes without rhyme or reason. Without rhythm or flow. Without structure or verse. Without even the "Roses are Red..." stuff. So try this instead: "Violets are Purple..." Beautifully and unpredictably purple, not blue. We're not blue either. So write on, everyone... Write on.

'Quest'-ions for Prayer and Further Reflection

- Who and what are you most fearful of right now? What are you trying to protect, possess, or preserve?
- In what ways are you figuratively 'locked up in your room' as a result?
- What types of walls are you constructing in your life to keep the 'undesirables' out of your circle?
- How are your critical judgments about other people and things manifested in the quality of your relationships, actions, beliefs, and feelings? How could this change toward more positivity?
- In what ways could you learn to let go of 'control' in so many aspects of your life? How can you live with more spontaneity and playfulness each day?

Our Quest for Belonging

Belonging:

- *To be part of something*
- *An object that is the property of someone*
- *Possessed by another*
- *To be properly and appropriately associated with something*
- *Included within something larger*

Re-Moat-Ly Inhospitable

YEARS AND YEARS AGO, the Ancient Near East celebrated long-standing traditions with respect to hospitality. Such treatment was expected in encounters with travelers, strangers, and aliens who came to one's door. Being hospitable entailed greeting the other. A greeting of friendship and peace. It involved creating a welcoming environment for the stranger. Exhibiting graciousness toward the other. It required providing food and beverage to the stranger. Shelter and rest. Protection and safety during the visitor's stay. It required reasonably provisioning the traveler for the next leg of his or her journey.

To be sure, it involved providing these things *for* the stranger. But it also required providing *of oneself to* the other, as well. The host might anoint the stranger with oil for onward blessings. The host might wash the dusty feet of the alien. The host might sit and eat with the stranger, rather than simply pushing a tray under the person's door at night. Most importantly, gracious generosity was undertaken for the other with no expectation of direct, immediate reciprocity. For, in these times, *all* might expect to be in the same precarious position one day—as a stranger dependent on a 'host' for surviving a long and arduous trek. It was true back then. It remains so today.

The United States is a country and a nation. It is a people. It is a landmass between the Atlantic and Pacific Oceans. It is a compiled history. It is a powerful force throughout the world. But, more than anything else, it is an idea. An ideal. An experiment. This idea, ideal, and experiment all center on the notions of human freedom and human liberty. In fact, our own iconic Statue of Liberty proclaims the following to incoming strangers: "Give me your tired, your poor, your huddled masses yearning to breathe free, the wretched refuse of your teeming shore. Send these, the homeless, tempest-tossed to me. I lift my lamp beside the golden door." In other words, Lady Liberty calls us to be freely hospitable to others.

Our great nation fought a terrible and deadly Civil War over the idea of freedom and our human rights of liberty. It did so initially in response to the South's beliefs that an over-reaching federal government forcibly threatened the rights of their citizens and states. It did so, as well, in response to the North's beliefs that the nation must remain indivisible—not allowing the South's cessation. In its later stages, the rationale shifted to the rights of African-American slaves—those bought and brought into savage bondage (not liberty) by our own U.S. citizens.

The North fought and won the Civil War to provide an unjustly and cruelly enslaved people with freedom and a measure of dignity. How ironic, then, that our country subsequently 'recombined' in a collective effort to violently steal sacred land and liberty from our only indigenous inhabitants: the Native Americans. It's as if we learned nothing from the Civil War's prior violence, fought in the name of shared freedom and liberty for all. "Give me your tired, your poor, your huddled masses yearning to breathe free . . . " How disgracefully inhospitable of us.

If history teaches us anything, it is this: human liberty and freedom are not about hoarding and claiming our own space. Our own property. Protecting our own 'voices' to the detriment of others. Claiming our own positions. Staking out our own rights at the expense of others. Our own 'truths' to the exclusion of others. Liberty is not about taking what's ours . . . then holding tightly to it. Keeping others out. Closing us in. Building walls. Protecting our precious purity. *None* of this constitutes 'belonging' to a community in any sense of the word.

But that's precisely the way it's been throughout the history of immigration to the United States. Let the record show that we didn't exactly welcome aliens and strangers from Ireland and Italy. From Eastern Europe. From China and Japan. With the former immigrants of generations-past having now long since settled in, we've more recently moved on to fear and loathe the latest groups. The new most despised people. Those from Mexico, Central America, and the Middle East to name a few. Wash. Rinse. Tumble Dry. Repeat Cycle. "Give me your tired, your poor, your huddled masses yearning to breathe free . . . " How disgracefully inhospitable of us.

Now, wide-open and chaotic borders without controls are not sustainable. Nor is a free-for-all as it regards immigration. But I *am* praying that the spiritual message of Lady Liberty takes greater hold on our soil and in our hearts. She knew and knows that we cannot wall ourselves off. That we cannot create an isolated, protective beachhead with piles and piles of sandbags in order to keep the water from creeping in. There is no moat long or wide enough to keep us safely ensconced in our paranoid 'castle'. We must, therefore, come to grips with that and with this: a free nation is only as strong as its most vulnerable and tenuous links within our society.

Each of us must feel as if we're wanted and belong here. We need each other in order to be truly free and prosperous. We need the inclusive diversity of *all* backgrounds, ethnicities, religions, ideas, histories, and contexts. Willing to incorporate them into the grand idea and experiment of human liberty and human rights. Then remaining open to be changed as Americans in the process. More importantly, to become 'richer' and more 'human' as God intended in the first place as a result.

The words on the Statue of Liberty capture this theme far more effectively than I ever could: "Send these, the homeless, tempest-tossed to me. I lift my lamp beside the golden door." Lady Liberty embodies the real 'heart' behind the spiritual notion of hospitality and belonging. She understands that hospitality toward others made sense not only in Ancient Near East cultures thousands of years ago. It still makes sense today. Perhaps more than ever before. So drain the moat. Build a bridge. Lift our lamp beside a golden door. Hospitably. Graciously. For we are *all* strangers, immigrants, and aliens during our lives. We *all* want to feel as if we belong.

Who Loves Me . . . Really?

What if God is Love? Not just love, but a powerful love? And what if the power of God's love truly defines the 'who, what, and why' of God? The kind of love that wants the best, the fullest, the most loving, liberated life for us. Not a jealous, possessive, obsessive, compulsive, and destructive kind of love. Not the kind of love that makes otherwise well-meaning people say: "Sorry for your loss, William. I guess that God needed another angel in heaven." "Sorry about his passing, Mary. But heaven is a little better place now with Ted there." "Sorry about your loss, Joe. I guess God loved your best friend too much." "Sorry about your pain, Sue. But God never gives you more than you can handle." "Sorry about this situation, Pete. God must really be angry with you. What did you do?"

No, not that kind of love. But an unconditional, non-stop, grace-filled love for us. That's right. For us. Powerful. Powerfully present and loving. Power-packed. I'm talking about the kind of love where God sits with you in your sorrow and pain and grief. The kind of love that brings loving people to your side when you hurt—and reminds you that you belong as 'family'. The kind of love that powers you to go on . . . sometimes to simply go on. To be open to tomorrow. The kind of love that brings unexpected blessings in the midst of pain. The kind of love that brings unexpected hope. The kind of love that attracts a new friend into your grieving space.

The kind of love that slowly brings a smile to your face when you remember someone lost. A smile that walks with your tears. Perhaps a smile before the tears for a change. A loving, happy memory. A new memory. A fresh memory coming back. That's a powerful love. It's there. God is there in the thick of things. Quietly transforming, healing, sustaining, and comforting you with all of God's power. Power that longs for your belonging.

The Peace of Deep Listening

At such a pivotal time in our world, we 'listen' to others less than ever. We receive in bites. In characters. In pictures. In bits. Sometimes just a little bit, actually. And we respond, in turn. Social media, TV, radio, and the Internet all talk at us. We talk back, in turn. But are we really listening? If not, it comes at a cost. For we cannot be 'connected' and cannot belong unless we're first connecting at deeper human levels. Human connection starts with listening. And that starts with each of us.

For the sake of an example, I'll picture myself as a co-worker, a friend, or a family member of another person. I greet her one morning asking, "How are you doing?" I probably expect the usual response from her: "I'm fine. Thanks for asking." Perhaps that's as deep as I want to go on this day, anyway. Or perhaps, I'm open to more. But she doesn't say, "I'm fine" this time. Instead she answers, "Not so good. Things are pretty bad, to be honest." Maybe she briefly complains about something or someone. Maybe she quickly laments about how she's just been treated a few minutes ago. And maybe my response is, "Wow. Sorry to hear that. I hope it gets better for you." Conversation done. While the interaction has been polite and respectful, it's not true listening. Instead, I've undertaken *'fly-by' listening*—superficially hearing her content. And it's certainly not going deeper.

A deeper dive might sound something like this in response to my friend's expressed plight. I might say, "I'm so sorry to hear this. I have some time now or later. I'd like to learn more about it if you're up to it." My new response is at least a start that sets the stage. Because I've now affirmed her importance as a person. I've signaled to her that I'm listening to the *content of her story at a deeper level*. This empowers her to share her story in more detail. In the process, I've become more connected. I actually join her in that story. I actually enter into it for a while.

But what if I were to go deeper, yet, in my listening? I can do so by *reflecting back her feelings*. For she's not just telling me a story. She also wants someone to join her feelings. Feelings like her being mad, sad, glad, afraid, overwhelmed, or anxious. I listen to her feelings when I verbally acknowledge what I perceive. I might say, "You sound angry." "I sense some real frustration on your part." "This seems really upsetting to you." "You're pretty mad about this, aren't you?"

When I listen for and reflect back her feelings, I might get her feelings wrong. Using phrases like "I seem to sense" or "Am I reading you correctly?" can help in this regard. And if I'm not reading her feelings correctly, I can let her know that it's OK for her to clarify. In any event, when I reflect back her feelings, I'm telling her that what's beneath the content of her story matters. That I care about her, not simply her story.

It's now time to challenge myself to listen even more deeply. I need to pay attention to *her affect, as I perceive it*—then reflect it back, where appropriate. It might sound something like this from me, "You sound really mad." "I can see the pensiveness and tightness on your face." "You're literally shaking." "Tell me more about your tears, please." Her affect is manifesting her feelings beneath. Both her feelings and her affect are unspoken. They're not expressed in words. But they matter greatly. When I acknowledge her affect, I 'tell' her that we're fully engaged in this moment together. My reflections also invite further dialogue. I'm now joining her more completely in empathy. As such, there's a far greater sense of mutual belonging.

When I listen more deeply to content, feelings, and affect, I open this final, most important possibility: I may hear the gift of *what's really underneath it all at a heart level*. Her anger, tears, and pensiveness may, in the end, have little to do with the 'presenting' issue that she raised today. Her opening story may simply be the pile of ice that lies above the surface. What sits beneath it is the deeper, heart-felt need. The one that's expressed only by my first listening more deeply in true human, spiritual engagement.

In so doing, I might learn that today is the anniversary of her spouse's death. Or the birthday of an estranged, long-time former friend of hers. Or that her experience today reminds her of being pushed away by others as a child. Left behind. Disrespected and marginalized. Or that she just got some extremely difficult medical news in her life a week ago. Perhaps these are the things tugging at her after all. Not the thing that brought on her initial response to you today.

Because I listened to her at a deeper, more thoughtful level, she brought her unconscious mind to her conscious mind. This is the beginning of addressing what matters most. And I was there to truly 'hear' her. To enter into her life for a moment. Not to advise or to fix or to solve her problem. Because I can't. Not to get in over-my-head or beyond my expertise. Because I shouldn't. But my deep, multi-layered listening *did* affirm her. It signaled that I care. That she matters. I may never know the extent of any real difference that I just made. But I may actually have. Deeply.

Belonging with an Upbeat Tempo

Jazz is a special kind of music. Perhaps unlike any other musical genre, in fact. Some argue that jazz is a dying art form. That its best days are behind it. I disagree. For its greatest attribute is its ability to move and change with the times. Its ability to evolve stems from the very nature of jazz itself. Jazz does the unexpected. Its rhythms, beats, and pauses are unanticipated and unpredictable. Major and minor keys often fluctuate regularly within a single song. The intonations vary. Jazz can be fused with other genres at times, as well. It mixes effectively with rock, blues, world music, and even classical forms.

Further, a great jazz tune literally makes the instruments 'sing', creating new and original sounds and moods with a trumpet, sax, piano, bass, or drums. It's not unheard of to hear a piano, electronic keyboard, vibes, and even an organ in a single album. And a piano, itself, can create both music and percussion by the power used on the keys. If that's not enough, jazz creates a call-response ambiance. A musician often plays a solo 'lick', followed by one from another member of the band. And the musicians draw energy from the audience along the way. Listening to jazz is not a spectator sport. It calls on our belonging and engagement. In some physical and emotional ways, we become part of the band. We belong.

But it doesn't end there. The great beauty of jazz lies far more in the soul and energy of the performers than in the song itself. The spirit of the band members influences the music tremendously and in remarkably spiritual ways. And while that spirit can convey itself from a jazz soloist, it finds its most elegant expression when the music played is actually played by a group. Whether it's a duo, trio, quartet, quintet, or a 'big band', jazz reaches a high note when artists come together to perform it.

Jazz reaches its highest note, however, when it is situational. When the band creates the music together from *within* the song. When the performance, itself, is situational. When the tune is driven less by a settled 'score' than by improvisation in the moment. Sure, it's important to have a song prepared. But jazz becomes 'spiritual' when the band members improvise during the song itself. Whether the jazz is bop, Dixieland, smooth, fusion, or classic, it reaches its truest form in its ability to evolve—both over time and just in time. Right now. When the song, itself, belongs to the moment.

As spiritual human beings, we play out our songs of living most often in groups. To be certain, we play it solo at times. And doing so is not a bad thing. But we need each other to get things done. To co-exist. To find relational happiness. To belong. So, in some ways, we're all like a jazz band. And, like a band, we write tunes. The sheet music is our roadmap. It provides structure to the 'music'. As it regards our co-existence in groups, we need to follow the norms of the group that we're in. If not, we can't produce music. The ensuing sound becomes some dissonant, discombobulated mess of a song.

And we need more than sheet music to guide us. Group norms are great as it were, but optimal co-existence and belonging require an informal hierarchy of some kind. Every band needs a leader. People living and working and existing together need something or someone that somehow transcends the individual whims and needs of each group member. Something or someone that mediates the potential conflicts between individual members. These things are important to co-existing with others, as we bring more than our talents, desires, and energy to the 'band'.

Unfortunately, we *also* bring our anxieties to our groups, as well. These anxieties may stem from past experiences of rejection. From how we're 'wired' internally. From what just happened to us the other day. From human development issues buried deeply within our psyches. From even diffused, unwarranted paranoia. Whatever the source, we bring our anxiety. But not just our anxiety. We also bring our efforts (whether conscious or unconscious) to reduce and control these anxieties as part of our participation with others in our familial, social, or work groups. These efforts take on numerous manifestations, translated into specific behaviors.

Our attempted anxiety-managing behaviors may come and go on a situational basis or can be fairly chronic and continuous. We may exhibit a few of them or all of them from time to time. For example, some of us simply close off and don't participate in groups. We shut down intellectually and emotionally. In order to deflect our anxiety, we simply 'leave' the group in a figurative sense. Others simply go along to get along. Agree with everything that's said. Some of us 'transfer' our anxieties to others within the group. We project them onto other members, who have no idea whatsoever what we're doing to them or even why.

In other cases we act-out. Create unnecessary drama within the group. In order to shine the light on ourselves. To get attention. Or to inexplicably sabotage our own best interests. Alternatively, we sometimes scapegoat others. Deflect blame. We play mental and emotional 'games' with others, trying to get ahead or to grab power. We might not even fully appreciate that we're doing these things. But we are. And our group behaviors aren't improvisation. They don't contribute to the band or to a sense of healthy 'belonging'. And what comes out isn't music. It's chaos.

When we co-exist with others in these kinds of unhealthy ways, the band doesn't function well. If everyone shuts down emotionally and simply goes along, the music is flat. It loses its very vibrancy. The song is lifeless, without creativity and spontaneity. Certainly not like good jazz. Conversely, sabotaging the group creates deep, threatening fissures within it. The group fractures. Out-groups are formed, as some members quit to form another group. In other words, they've cut themselves off from the larger group. Instead of collaborating, they're now competing. No one feels as if they belong anymore.

Perhaps even worse, some groups splinter into subsets while technically 'staying together'. Different sub-groups plot and scheme against others within the group. Someone may emerge with 'cult-like' power to challenge the band's current leader. Then the 'you-know-what' hits the fan. Trumpets glare. Saxes are smashed. Taken to the extreme, one of the splintered clusters may actually mutiny in ways that actually overthrows the larger group. When this happens, everybody in the band separates. Never to reunite. Lots of baggage and hard feelings that calcify over time. Then nobody contributes to the band anymore. And what comes out isn't music. It's chaos.

You might argue that my analogy of a jazz band is good at least in theory. But that life isn't really a band. For we're all soloists in the end. We're individuals making our own way in this world. However, that would be shortsighted. For, in truth, we are highly inter-connected and interactive as people. At home with our families. On the job with our co-workers. In our places of worship. Within our social groups. In our volunteer organizations. With our closest group of friends. Participation and 'being' with others is written into our very human DNA. But we often don't 'play well' with others, for reasons both conscious and unconscious. We fracture relationships. We separate from others.

But here's the thing. Real life dysfunction isn't like quitting a jazz band for another gig somewhere else. Not at all. In fact, it's much worse indeed. For when we figuratively or literally walk out on our families, friends, and co-workers, we haven't just ruined a song. We've ruined lives. And hearts. And souls. And homes. And workplaces. So, living with others isn't like a jazz band in many critical ways. Being and belonging with others in healthy, spiritual ways is not like spinning off some song . . . or performing an incredible show. It's way more important than that.

However, we *can* learn something from playing great jazz, I believe. Jazz comes far less from the minds of its composers than is the case in most other music genres. Instead, it comes from the composers' inner souls. Jazz speaks musically from the heartbreaks, blues, pains, rejection, hopes, and exuberance of resilient, creative hearts. Real life lived in the trenches. As such, the best jazz that you'll ever hear isn't played in giant 'sterile' concert halls. It's experienced in small, off-the-beaten-path clubs on the margins of Main Street. Not in stadium seating. But around small tables. Where the interactions of the band are mirrored by the interactions of audience groups sitting together. Close to each other and close to the band itself. Spiritual 'belonging' is like that. Our ability to live and work and play together speaks to bringing our whole selves to the endeavor.

We do this 'bringing together' not by masking our own insecurities and our individual hurts in anxious, secretive, or acting-out ways. Rather, we do so by channeling our pasts and our souls in creative, conscious, and collaborative ways. In a true call-response melody. In sufficiently structured, but honest, improvised, and situational ways. Where everybody has a part to play. At the best times in the song. Sometimes as a solo interlude. But always within the context of the music itself. The band itself. That's belonging and behaving with an upbeat tempo. One, two, three, four . . . .

The Case For Love

For the sake of argument, let's say that I've happened upon another person after work one day. I'm walking to catch my train home when I see him out of the corner of my eye. The person is sitting with his back to a building's exterior wall on a sidewalk bordering a busy city street. He looks at me as I'm walking by and calls out, "God bless you, stranger." Then he holds out a cup towards me in a way that appears to be asking for money. It looks as if the stranger is homeless. Because he has trash bags of clothes and belongings at his side on the ground. At first, I'm inclined to walk right by him. Or even speed up to avoid his glance and get out of the rain as quickly as possible. But I think otherwise and slow my pace. Then I stop and give the man a few dollars. Is this love?

How would it be different if, instead of a homeless stranger, I stopped by a friend's house and gave him some money to assist him in paying an unexpected hospital bill? And instead of walking away like I did with the homeless stranger, I stayed with my friend for a few hours to listen to him and talk? How would it be even more different if I dropped what I was doing to pick up a family member when she called to inform me that her car had broken down many miles away? While, in both instances, I stopped everything in order to help another person in an emergency, are these necessarily examples of love? The aforementioned scenarios and their attendant questions help to frame the fundamental question here: when is human generosity *also* human love? If so, what kind of love?

Let's get a bit creative in this regard. What if we were to look at this as a legal case of sorts? You know, like the People's Court on TV . . . but this time, the Love Court instead. If I were to take my examples to the court and argue my previously described actions towards strangers, friends, and family were 'love', I'd have to show *Legal Standing*. In other words, I would need to demonstrate that I was harmed or impacted by my purportedly loving actions. In other words, I'd have to prove that I had something legitimately at stake as a result of my actions.

The concept of Legal Standing is to a court case what *Intent* is to our notion of human love. Dropping a few dollars in a stranger's tin cup on the streets might constitute love . . . or not, depending on my motives and intent. I may have deposited the money out of guilt. Or as a result of personal embarrassment over my own relative wealth compared to the stranger's poverty. Or I may have given the money simply in order to get out of there quickly. Or to make myself feel better in the moment. The same would be true as it regards my giving money to my friend or rescuing my family member in a moment of need. In order to love another, I have to have real standing. Not legal standing. But standing nonetheless. Positively 'intentional' standing in the Court of Love.

In a legal sense in the Love Court, *Questions of Fact* could also influence my case. Evidence of my past practices would matter. For example, if my sudden acts of generosity to the stranger, friend, and family member were merely one-time, inspired anomalies, they're hardly factual evidence of my loving intent. The specific situations involved would matter too. If I gave up something big in order to generously provide for another, it would constitute evidence of my positive intent. So if I missed my train home from work because I took time to actually talk to the homeless stranger, it would be good. Or if I took the stranger to a deli and bought him a sandwich, even better. Or better yet if I sat with him while he ate his meal. Or even shared a meal with him.

Taken further, if I could submit *multiple* previous examples of my outward generosity, I might cite it as *Precedent* to the Love Court. You know, allowing the judge to consider past cases of clearly loving actions in my life. I might even claim that I'm an *Originalist*. In a Constitutional sense, this means that I interpret the law according to the original intent of the Constitution's framers hundreds of years ago. In my case, I would argue that the essence of my love has already been long established. And that my actions have therefore clearly and consistently met the test of love. In the same way that love is continuous over time, so are my actions of generosity. Case closed, your honor. The prosecution rests.

But all this legal argumentation begs the real *Question of Law* before the court. And here is that question: what is the actual state of my heart in my actions? I can argue that I love someone. But if this love has been driven by my hormones, the ancient Greeks would call my love Eros. An exotic, passionate kind of love. If I'm helping a friend and tell him, "I love you, buddy," the ancients would call my love Philia. The love of human friendship. If I am helping someone based on my love of self, the ancients would call this Philautia. If my love of self is healthy, that Philautia love is shared with others along the way. Outwardly projected.

All these types of love are, in fact, love. They all demonstrate generosity in some way. A giving of ourselves. Whether in passion, friendship, or healthy self-assurance. The judge in the Court of Love might still find my heart wanting, though. He or she might not rule in favor of love. For the truest meaning of love is what the ancient Greeks would call *Agape*. This is a broad, spiritual, and selfless love. Agape Love is borne in our ability to freely give of ourselves. It is the purest form of human love. No strings attached. No expectations for reciprocity.

Agape love wants the best for another human being, no matter the cost to oneself in the process. It's focused first and always on another. In this sense, it's entirely other-centered. This kind of love is hard to give. Really hard. Sometimes seemingly impossible, to be honest. It's driven from a core of feeling first loved ourselves. Of being assured and secure in our own being. Of being centered in the present.

But it's also based on an intense faith. Faith that life is not a zero-sum game. That God provides for us all. That God loves us all. Based on an inherently optimistic faith in the future. That helping another selflessly accrues to all creation down the road. It's also grounded in the belief that nothing is too small or too large to give another. For it all matters. Small things can become big things tomorrow. Or the next day. Or the one after that. Finally, agape love is driven by the assurance that it is only in giving freely that we receive the greatest joy, gratitude, and happiness.

In the end in the Court of Love, the case turns on our *Hearts*. As it always has and always will. Facts and evidence do matter. So does precedent. So do procedures and our motions. But, in this instance, God is the ever-present Originalist in the courtroom. That's right. God did not draft a Constitution. But God did something far more important. God drafted all human beings for all times. And God's intent was always Agape Love as the greatest kind of love for another person. This intent is changeless and timeless. While *we* may rest our case or even settle out of court, God never settles. God never rests. For God's love for us is the truest, purest one: Agape Love. And God's case for it is never dismissed.

Salt and Light

In the 2nd Testament of the Bible, Jesus Christ referred to the 'Kingdom of God' numerous times. Some say that he did so more often than anything else that he talked about. Most would agree that this Kingdom was pivotal in everything Christ did while on earth some two thousand years ago. Yet Jesus didn't really define the term for us, and we're left to piece it together after-the-fact. Based on the broader context of Christ's mission and message. As such, there is some understandable confusion about what the Kingdom really is or will become. About when it will finally come into its fullness. Whether it is for individuals or for us collectively. And, even if collective, who is called to be part of it, exactly.

One of the greatest problems with the term is the very word, 'Kingdom'. Its derivative word 'King' conjures up all kinds of uneasiness within those of us sensitive to gender and history. Ancient societies were often unmistakably and undeniably male-oriented in terms of rights, privileges, and power. Women and children were second-class citizens in many fundamental ways. If we're honest, they still are today in important aspects of our lives. So 'Kingdom' conveys a sense of patriarchy and maleness. It thereby excludes others by the very nature of the word's nomenclature. Unfortunately, it also implies a feudal sense of exclusiveness—in terms of those belonging to it. Being part of a 'Kingdom' implies that we reside within set boundaries or territories. That we're under the protection of the King, to whom we pay homage. In all likelihood, paying taxes and fees in return for our cloistered safety.

Some strive to resolve this by changing the label to the 'Reign of God'. This gets rid of the gender issues, but it should leave us wanting for something better. For 'Reign' implies regal power based on long-standing tradition. It's easy to picture a Reign as a thing of control, privilege, pomp, and lavish ceremony. In turn, we can picture ourselves as subserviently and submissively 'belonging' to the reign relative to the rule of another person actually in power. And our obeying the letter of the law in a covenant for royal protection. So while Reign resolves one aspect of our problem, it doesn't significantly change the regrettable spirit of it.

What if there's another way? We could use the words, 'Plan of God' as a substitute. For surely God has a plan for us all as part of God's loving creation act. I mean, what reputable creator or developer attempts to construct a building without a set of detailed, finished plans? An architect's renderings or drawings, layouts, and specifications. Ergo, a plan. God is the grand architect. Christians believe that Jesus Christ is the incarnate and divine embodiment of God and God's plan. That Christ is the completion and communication of the architect's plan.

If we go in this direction, it's important to ask this: what part do we play, as humans, in the plan? Well . . . we are the laborers in the process. We take this embodied plan and we work to complete the construction of it. Like carpenters, we help to build the structures to specifications as best as we can understand them—grounded in a firm foundation already laid for us. Day-by-day, we add bricks and mortar to it. If we're true to our faith, we do our small parts with hearts of love, faith, charity, and belonging.

This image of builders and carpenters is helpful in many ways. For it reminds us that we are not the main architects of our destiny. We help to shape it and build it, but we do not truly create it. We leave the 'big picture' to the Transcendent One. At the same time, however, the image poses this important problem: it emphasizes too much our principal value in *doing* something as our 'ticket of admission' to belonging here. In acting on and in the world. In turn, it fails to properly highlight our role in simply 'being' something in the first place.

As a result of this deficiency, we need to keep searching for something better to complete the picture. And Dietrich Bonhoeffer may have provided the answer. Bonhoeffer was an iconic 20th Century German pastor, author, and theologian. He was also an active, ardent resister of Adolph Hitler and his brutal Nazi regime in Germany. Bonhoeffer was arrested, jailed, and subsequently executed in 1945 towards the end of World War II and the dismantling of the Third Reich by the Allied Forces.

In his famous book, *The Cost of Discipleship*, Bonhoeffer calls forth the teachings of The Beatitudes in the 2nd Testament Biblical Gospel of Matthew. He also reminds his readers of the importance of not just Christ's blessings. But of Christ's challenge to us to be *Salt and Light*, as well. Bonhoeffer clarifies an important distinction between what we should *be*, on the one hand, and what we should *do*, on the other. He argues that we are *already* Salt and Light as part of our having been created and called by God. We have these things within us to begin with.

As salt, we have the potential to add seasoning and taste to life around us. In fact, that's what we're made of, and we need to share it with others. As light, we have the potential to add visibility to others. To help light the way. In fact, that's what we're made of, and we need to share it with others. Salt and Light cannot be ignored, held-back, or hidden. The very nature of salt and light demands their actual use in service to others. If we attempt to serve without our 'salt', this essential element within us loses its taste. And we might as well throw the salt away. If we attempt to serve without 'light', we extinguish the light within us. It loses its very essence.

This isn't to say that our failure to be Salt and Light equates with going to Hell, whatever that is. But it *does* imply that we don't fully exist as humans without recognizing the importance of these crucial elements. The elements fundamentally belong to and are within us. Salt and Light are, therefore, at our core as spiritual people. These qualities are, in turn, to be used and shared. In so doing, we become more fully human. In this way, our very *beings* are the bedrock of God's plan for us. And we act as builders, using and sharing these innate characteristics. These gifts of God to us.

Doing so with trust and faith means that we're comfortable knowing that we'll never actually see the structure completed on this side of eternity at least. And comfortable in knowing that the structure we've labored to build will never have a roof on it. For nothing should be laid on top of it to close off the sky. Nothing should enclose us who reside and belong together within. Nothing should serve to entomb our salt, the very salt that is made to season and add flavor to life. Nothing should dampen the light that we evoke from within our souls. We were made to live out-of-doors anyway. For we belong in the real world, according to God's plan. This plan is God's spiritual hope for all humanity: being God's own Salt and Light in the world.

'Quest'-ions for Prayer and Further Reflection

- In what ways does your walk of faith most mirror and contrast with the inclusive love of Christ?
- Do you sometimes lose the collective, communal elements of your faith in the face of your focus on your individual spiritual status and

future? If so, in what ways and at what costs to you and others as a result?

- What barriers can you begin to break down right now in the spirit of grace, fellowship, and community?
- What positive and negative behaviors do you bring to your relationships with family, friends, co-workers, community members, and faith circles? How do your behaviors vary according to the specific group you're with at the moment? And why?
- How actively do you 'listen' to yourself and to others in your daily walk? How deep are you willing to go?

Our Quest for Truths

Truth:

- *In accordance with facts and data*
- *Supported by convincing evidence*
- *Something accepted as the reality*
  - *The adopted standard*
- *A judgment or belief adhered to*

Un-Shelved, Un-Stacked, and Un-Bound

THE HUMAN QUEST FOR truth is akin to walking into a large public library. A stately, mysterious old place. On a cold, rainy, bone-chilling night. While searching for a lost dog, based on some sign that you saw posted on a nearby street lamp. With a cute dog picture on the posting and a caption that reads, 'Have you seen me? $250 reward for information or return. No questions asked'. Then asking yourself, "I wonder where this dog might be? I have nothing else going tonight. So I might as well find the dog and collect the reward money. I could use a few extra bucks in my pocket, anyway. Maybe the poor little pooch is in the library. I'll go in and check it out. If nothing else, it'll get me out of the elements for a while."

Before entering this old, mysterious library, I briefly stand outside and look upon it. Even though I'm shivering in the rain and cold, biting wind. For it's hard to miss this place. It holds one's attention. It stands out in its immensity and its proportion . . . as compared with the small shops and stores all around it. It also stands on its reputation. As *the* place of learning and knowledge in town. Where truth is housed and shelved. Where people go to find things out. Or to get out from under their misconceptions. Where they become enlightened. Made smart. Or simply made.

If the library's reputation isn't enough, its outward appearance clearly is. One need only look upon it to know. You can know a book by its cover, I'm told. And this place has a real 'cover'. For the library has the grandest entrance ever made. Huge pillars mark the outside doors. Approached by the grandest stairway ever laid. Stairs of pure gold and granite. Each step a priceless beauty found. Secure beneath one's feet. But that's not all. There's more.

Before the doors, two fountains sit. One for this side. One for that. From these fountains spring a misty foam. A giant arch of streams galore. Forming rainbows in the sunlight's glow. Or sparkling beams in moonlight's rows. The waters spring from creatures' mouths. Mystic beings that love to spout. All below some marble carvings. Of gods and kings and queens observing. As if to watch the various souls, who stare and gawk while I climb the mighty stairs. The stairway to this grand old place. Await the opening of the doors. To enter in and to be transformed. Beneath the alcove greeting all.

The outside entrance finally reached. Another treat for weary feet. For soggy feet. Once inside, I've reached the place. Of knowledge and of truth. A place of books. Of volumes. Of tomes. Of stacks and shelves. And many rows. A many storied place. Many floors. Lots of nooks and crannies. Lots of spaces. Firmly held by gothic, granite walls. Marble pillars. Shiny granite floors. With light supplied by slender slats. Of iron and of glass. A window's spot. Throughout. A thousand panes of glass. A thousand pounds of lead. Lead that holds the glass in place. Throughout this meandering place. Across this winding, monstrous space.

And many statues grace the walls. Adorn the halls. Stand guard for falls. Beveled, chiseled stone. No matter what the form. Formed or freely flowing. Tall and small, so many sizes. Big and brawny, so many slices. Straight and curvy, so many splices. Real and make-believe, so many prices. Lots and lots of figures. Too many, in fact. Almost piled atop each other. Like a crowd of people simply waiting. Watching. Nary an empty place. Almost not an open space. These many figures. So much to see. Even if grounded and lifeless. Of people. Of gargoyles. Of myths and creatures. Of dragons with features. Like Roman gods. Nearly lifelike, yet cast in bronze or rock. Not to live or move. But to stand like sentries. Guarding what we cannot know. For these sentries do not talk. No, not at all. No, not a sound. So we'll never know. We can only guess.

As if this place, this library, was weak, the makers strove to speak. In loud and towering ways. They built some doors. Lots of doors. Inside doors. Outside doors. And in-between. Doors to enter. Doors to exit. Doors, doors, doors. Everywhere. And framed. Heavy doors without a doubt. To leave no doubt. Not a shred of doubt. Steel doors, iron doors. Massive doors. Wide and tall and very strong. Swung slowly, nearly imperceptibly. As if to say, "I'll take my time."

The heavy doors are sure adorned. With grooves and molds and lines. Sometimes shiny, sometimes worn. Sometimes glittering. Sometimes torn. Some are square. Some are rounded. Some have windows through which to stare. But doors they are. They do their stuff. With authority and pride. As if to say, "Hello." As if to say, "Goodbye." As if to say, "Pass through." As if to say, "Come in, so long. What's keeping you so long?" "This way here, that way there. No, not this room, that room. The one in there." Or "Hurry up now. Time's a wasting. I don't have long. We're closing soon."

Oh, and the accouterments. The many splendored things throughout. Adorned beyond each door. Walk through this door. Or out that one. Be greeted by a vast array. Of paintings that are large and small. Wide and tall. Bold and cold. Artwork of the masters. As well as the unknowns. Of artists far and wide. This much is surely known. Colors splash. Colors dash. Colors dart and dance. On canvas sheets framed not by chance. Nothing random. Not a chance. The oils and sketches true and pure. Pure creativity abounds.

As if this artwork needed more, the works are lit by lights galore. The chandeliers hang nicely low. To add a sheen of light below. Cut crystal glass encase the bulbs, to add a touch of class throughout. And on the window ledges tall, sit potted plants that seem to call. As if this weren't enough for sure, the floors do add a final touch. Patterns, patterns everywhere. Designs too fine for feet to tread. Tempting feet to sit instead. Or lay and rest. Or stay the course. Goodness, gracious so much grandeur. Not just one room, but them all.

Not just one floor, but far too many, really. One can see the ceiling from the first floor. From the center of it all. Each floor adorned with stacks of books. More than one can count. More than two could count. Stacks on stacks. Filled with books. In every row. In every nook. Each stack nicely labeled. To guide the patrons and keep them stable. Wrought iron railings to guard the drop-offs. To save the patrons should they doze-off.

Empty spaces filled with tables, long and regal, made of maple. And chairs with hard backs, some soft backing. Some feel sturdy, some seem lacking. In spots, a fireplace that does not function. An aging lift that's lost its gumption. It's an elevator of course. That's lost its course. And simply sits. In remembrance of what once was moving. Now sulks and simply needs some soothing.

But the strangest things of all are not the art and not the doors. Not the flowers, windows, floors. Not the volumes nicely stored. Not the splendor of the rooms. Not the curtains or the lights. Not the stairways strewn throughout. Not the books so tossed about. No indeed. It's not these things. Instead, it's the dome that stands above. So high. So tall. Atop a single set of spiral stairs. Not just any kind of dome. No ordinary dome. To be sure. And that's for sure. A regal dome. Imposing dome. A sparkling dome. Beautiful. Undeniably sure. *In its day*. Once upon a time. A long, long time ago. Seems like only yesterday. The once-majestic dome. Atop a spiral staircase. Many narrow, winding steps. That lead the way. Around, around so many bends. Upward. Toward the dome. Toward the sky.

And right below the dome there is a place. A place to stand and gaze. To simply stand. To look down. To peer around. Discern the sky and clouds and stars. To see the sun. To see the moon. If not to gaze, to simply stand in place. To stop the race. To rest the pace. To claim this place. So much to see. So much to say. A place to stand or sit and stay. In its day. In its day. But something happened, you see. Bad and sad, not glad.

The years went by. The time did pass. The seconds waned. The once-proud dome was left behind. In disrepair. In real despair. The once-clear glass did lose its cast. It's now a streaky mess. A filmy blaze. And, over time, the cracks appeared. First a few. Then a lot. From end to end. Like wiry snakes. That slithered to and fro. And pulled the glass. Apart from its leaded, leaden frames. Like a tug-o-war to see who'd win. The Battle for the Dome.

Waged for years and years and years. Amidst a thousand tears. Amidst neglect. Amidst respect. Amidst regret. Amidst a thousand fears. So this once-proud dome now simply sits. Upon the roof. Not much to see. No place to go these days. The sunlight barely makes its way inside. What once was clear is now opaque. What once was bright is now a fade. One can hardly see a thing. Beyond the hazy dome. A fog of sorts. A cloudy mess.

And water seeps right through the glass. Through the many, many cracks. Drip. Drip. Drip. When it rains, it almost pours. As if it breached the glass in utter scorn. As if to say, "I won. I won. It took a while. You fought it well. But, in the end, I won. I won. I always knew I would. Win, I mean. I always knew I would. For all things fall before me. For I am 'truth', however torn and leaky. I'm in the Dome, however shot and streaky. I'm disguised by disrepair. By deep despair. It seems unfair. Silly folks. This was my plan. A clever plan. A guiling plan. A long-term plan. For in the cracks and film and wear, I come. To stay. To rule. I am the window to the world. The Truth. Your truth. For I'm the only way. It's my way. Or it's no way. So walk those winding stairs. So come and stand with me. So come and stay by me. So come and learn the truth from me."

Far too often, our human quest for truth is like the old library and the dated dome that sits atop it. In our search for spiritual surety, we turn to our 'sources'. We look for truth. Sometimes for only one 'truth'. And then we stop. We may actually think that we've found it, in fact. Perhaps it's sitting inside a warm, majestic library. Or under a stately, but leaky dome. We think we can find it in a place. Or in a single experience. In a book. Even a sacred book. In the stacks. Or in the shelves. Or on our smartphones. Online through a web search. We think we can find it. Then book it. Mark it down as real and get on with our lives. When things go awry, we can check the source. Get the answer. And make it 'home'.

The comfort of our 'safe places' of truth feels helpful on the quest. Especially in times of figurative plagues, floods, storms, darkness, hunger, thirst, and doubt. If all else fails, we can climb the spiral stairs to the perch just under the dome. And look down upon it all. To gain some temporary perspective. Or look up to the sky through the dome's glass. Even if trying to see through a hazy, opaque skylight. But here's the thing, though: it's easy for the library to become a prison. One in which we never find the 'lost dog' that we came into the library to find in the first place. Or one in which we never earn the reward for actually finding it. So the dog stays lost, either literally or figuratively. And so do we.

But, more importantly, staying in the library isn't really a quest for truth at all. For we can't actually quest for truth without an ongoing practice and discipline of openly seeking. Going forth. We need to seek and to actively pursue *many* potential truths. This is because a quest implies our full engagement as a person, a being. It's likely to be an active, encompassing experience. It's undoubtedly an adventure. It most definitely involves some risk. It's a hunt, of sorts. And it may be a long one. Probably difficult and challenging at times.

Further, the truths that we quest for as human 'beings' are different for each of us. And finding what we most seek might be hard. That which we seek may be hidden. Buried. Admittedly, there may be clues along the way. All kinds of things can be helpful in the quest. But no one map or book or set of instructions will work for everyone. In fact, our biggest risk is this: that in the process of our quests for truth, we *bind* ourselves to something . . . like a book that's tightly bound. Anchored nicely in a stack of books on a shelf. A shelf that neatly separates the true from the untrue. In this, we think we've found the answer.

It's easy. But it's a trick. For we haven't found anything really. Instead, we've gotten stuck in the tight creases of a book. And the bookshelves are nothing more than impermeable walls that separate us from others and ourselves. Barriers to deeper discovery. Bars to our innate curiosity and openness. And the crusty, mildewed dust on the books almost imperceptivity seeps into our very beings. It's all happening. But we just don't know it. In truth, it's nothing more than false security. A façade. Not a whole lot more satisfying than our failing to take the quest in the first place. Like a book with nothing but a hole in it where the pages should have been.

Books should be bound. So that pages will stay in place. So the books don't unravel. The stitching is precise. The bindings are firm. Everything holds together if the job's done right. But *we're* not books. We're people. We're spiritual beings. And ironically enough, we need to actually *unbind* ourselves if we're ever to quest for truths. Because our spiritual beings lie not in a tome. Or a tomb. Or even within an old and stately, comfortable library. Nor atop a perch beneath a leaky dome. Even when, atop the staircase, we think we see it all beneath us. For it's not beneath us at all. It's not outside of us. It's within us.

Here's the paradox of the quest for truths. While we must look first within us to find them, we can't truly know them until we look outside. We have to step back from 'us' once in a while. Actually get out of the library. Put our books down every so often. Unbind ourselves and unbind our souls. And take the quest. It will end where it started, in us. But, by virtue of our getting on our feet and walking, it will surely secure the truest treasure: a sense of perpetual seeking what is true. The true unity of our hearts, minds, bodies, and our souls. Then, and only then, can we do more than simply exist. Then, and only then, can we extraordinarily live our lives in their fullest. Then, and only then, can we extraordinarily 'be' in the many truths that we find along the way.

Deductive Unreality

In our search for truths, it's important to make some distinctions. There's a real and substantive difference between the word 'truth' and the word 'facts'. Seeking truths should necessarily involve embracing real facts and data to support these truths. For it's impossible to hold valid truths without rational and thoughtful support underneath. Furthermore, there are real differences in how we reach these truths.

We reach them *deductively* when we reason from the general-to-the-specific. We start with a premise or a hypothesis. Then we evaluate and test it with facts or observations. Conversely, we think *inductively* when we go from the specific-to-the-general. We discover broad truths based on the facts and observations that we've gathered. Both deductive and inductive approaches are valid. What's invalid, however, is *Deductive Unreality*. This happens when we make generalizations or create truths, while simultaneously ignoring or muzzling inconvenient facts that don't support these 'truths' . . . or the people who espouse them.

Deductive unreality becomes spiritually harmful when those who claim 'truth' are in positions of power over our lives and over the expression of our identities as human beings. Or when we cede our own inherent power to others. For when others try to define *their* truths as truths for all, it devalues us. It disempowers us. It debilitates us. It kills our souls. It extinguishes the light that God has placed within us. The snuffing out of our light often happens gradually. Sometimes without our even knowing it. And by the time we finally come to understand our predicament, we've already ceded our critical thinking and truth seeking to someone else. It can happen in our jobs. Within our families. On the streets and in our communities. And in our churches. Yes, even in our churches if the point of it all is blind conformance.

We would all be wise to be vigilant in this regard. And to look for the subtle or obvious signs around us in the sphere of truths and facts. We know that something is wrong when others try to confuse or obfuscate facts—rather than actively seeking and honestly verifying them. We know that something's wrong when those who claim truth act in ways that reject, attack, and vilify those who disagree with them. Or when thoughtful discourse is reduced to the least common denominator and the fewest words possible. When we're asked to memorize something and to never forget it.

We know something's wrong when we're given precious 'talking points' to spew out, yet we don't have the wherewithal to explain why these 'truths' are actually true. We know that real truth isn't sought when the 'truth' is wrapped with emotive, inflammatory words to polarize the debate. To separate the real believers from the troublemakers outside the trusted clan. We should also worry about 'truth' when the macro is reduced to the micro with regularity. This happens when the purveyors of 'truth' default to anecdotal, one-off examples rather than broader, fact-based information and trends.

We should be concerned when people purposefully confuse terms or have to subsequently 'walk them back' with any regularity. Or when someone has to subsequently 'redefine' them in order to clarify resultant confusion. Or to reinterpret their own 'terms' and words in ways that they didn't intend in order to confuse us about their real meaning. We should also worry when those who profess to hold the truth move conversations along quickly. As if to cut off debate. As if to discourage our questions. As if to push things through in order to quickly wrap things up.

Finally, we should be fearful when the holders of 'truth' create or convey a sense of chaos and destabilization around us. Tell us that we're under attack by sinister or evil forces that are trying to confuse or hurt us. For when we gravitate to these sellers of fear and loathing, we're unwittingly catering to our own perceived needs for personal safety. We're seeking protection and calm, not truth. Never mind that the chaos was created purposefully and precisely to make us fearful in the first place . . . and then draw us into *their* circle of safety.

This is especially pernicious when we subsequently circle the wagons around us. Then demonize those who disagree with us by calling them hateful names or using derogatory labels. We make these outsiders objects of our disdain at our own peril. For *we* become increasingly desensitized in the process. Our God-given spirituality and humanity begin to crumble away. Rapidly, in fact. All this said, there is nothing inherently wrong with deductive thinking. There's nothing wrong with creating a supposition, then testing it against reality. In the light of real facts.

It becomes dangerous, however, when the hypothesis is already given as undeniably 'true'. No matter what the facts tell us otherwise. This isn't truth seeking. Nor is it deductive. And it's not reality. But if you accept it as real, the windy sound that you'll hear is your very soul being sucked right out of you. Worse yet, you might have already been erroneously convinced that it's not your soul leaving your body. That would be truly and patently false. But that would also be real. Scary, but very real, indeed. Deductively speaking, that is.

This is Not a Test

The Biblical character of Job had everything. I mean everything. He had it made, as they say. He had a wife. Had children. Animals and livestock. Servants. Land. The whole works. And he was righteous. The 1st Testament book of the Bible says that he was blameless. A good man. The whole package in a guy. And everything was going his way in life. The good life. The whole deal. A smooth 'gig' on cruise control. Living large in every sense of the word. Nothing to fear other than fear itself.

But then it happened. The Bible states that God got into it with the Devil. Satan 'baited' God into testing Job. For the Devil believed that Job would curse God if everything Job had was taken away from him. If things started to go 'south' on him. If life turned on him. God didn't believe that Job would turn, even if life turned upside down for him. So God said "OK" to Satan. God let Satan ruin everything in Job's life. And I mean everything. Job lost his children. His livestock. His health. Total devastation. In fact, Job's wife encouraged Job to curse God for letting all of this go down. I mean, how does God let something this awful happen to such good people, anyway?

Then along came Job's friends. Three of them. They purportedly came to console and comfort Job. They messed up though. They did a poor job of it, in fact. Instead of simply being there for and with Job in his suffering, they got into sermonizing. And moralizing. And judging Job. They tried to convince him that it was his *own* sinfulness that had caused all of his sufferings. They articulated the thinking of many in the Bible's 1st Testament: that God punishes us right here for our sins. Not necessarily only later after we die. It was commonly believed that bad things happen to bad people in *this* life. Stuff like Job was going through. If you do bad, you get bad.

His friends called on Job to repent. To beg for God's forgiveness for Job's own sins and those of his family. For this entire mess must surely be from God's own hands. Retribution, in fact. But Job refused to admit his sinfulness. He continued to defend himself. More importantly, though, he refused to curse God. Instead, he entreated God for some meaning in his suffering. What's this all about, God? The Biblical account has God answering Job not with statements, but with a *series of questions*. Ones like, "Where were you when I created the world? How can you possibly understand the things that I can as God? Are you trying to be right at my expense, Job? Who do you think you are, anyway?" Probably not the answers that Job was looking for, to be honest.

Likely bewildered even further by God's response, Job backed down. He stood humbled before God. And he apologized for questioning God in the space of the unknowable mysteries of God. He expressed despising himself now and he repented. And what did God do in response? God repudiated Job's friends for their own bad counsel to Job. Job responded, in turn, by praying for his wayward friends. The three well-intentioned guys that showed up and then messed up. In the midst of it all, Job prayed for others.

The story of Job is recounted many, many times as part of the practice of Christian and Jewish faiths. And there's a lot to learn from telling the story as part of our worship and daily living. But Job is too often interpreted in ways that create potential problems. First, God comes off as the 'bad guy' in some ways. It makes God look like a schemer. A deal maker with evil forces. What's worse, it creates the notion that God is testing Job with extreme measures. As if God needs to give Job an exam to find out what Job's truly made of on the inside. How incredible is that? I would imagine that God already knew what Job was all about. Not sure why a test was even necessary.

To make matters even more problematic, our common interpretations make God an all-powerful abuser of sorts, even if only via indirect complicity with Satan's plan. Even if God merely stood back and allowed it to happen in the first place. As if God is saying, "Hey, I'll let the devil push this guy to the limits of suffering and see how he handles it." You know, like God is in the stands at Rome's Coliseum watching Job confront the hungry lions. And telling the guy next to him, "My money is on Job. He'll be the last one standing . . . (gulp) I hope."

Worse even yet, it makes God a heartless, dismissive bully at best. As if God tried to humiliate a suffering Job by angrily putting Job in his place *in the very midst* of Job's pain and pleading outreach to God. By refusing to answer Job's cries, other than by reinforcing Job's insignificance before God's majesty. Because, of course, we mere humans can never really understand things in the first place. And God doesn't like to be questioned anyway. In all these ways and in many others, the common interpretations we give to the story of Job create a 'bad look' for God, I'm afraid.

Let's take this even a step further for the sake of argument. When we read the Biblical story of Job according to our many traditional interpretations, we risk *internalizing* our shame and unworthiness. And we attribute our suffering to God's hands. The old saying goes that, if we live long enough, we'll all taste suffering. Sometimes, though, we don't have to live very long at all before the suffering comes. It sometimes comes so tragically to little children. And to infants. In other words, we're *all* tested with suffering 'from the jump'. It's a universal, equal-opportunity component of human life.

And this suffering isn't dished out by some kind of petty God who picks out this person or that one in order to drop the heavy rock on him or her. Bad stuff happens to everyone, sometimes even randomly during the walk of human life. So if this really isn't about God's character and not about our own, per se, what's the story of Job all about in the end? Here's another way to look at it. Perhaps the Biblical Book of Job is really about our *shared* suffering. About what we can learn about us and each other in the face of inevitable suffering. And about re-defining the idea of 'healing' when we do suffer.

For Job's heart wasn't opened by God's questions back to him. In fact, Job ultimately stepped back, apologized, and repented his inquiries of God. Instead, Job was 'awakened' spiritually by the *suffering of others* in the midst of his own. Job's heart was moved by the suffering of his three friends. By the very friends who had come to comfort him. When God rebuked Job's friends for their bad counsel to and their judgment on Job, Job prayed for them.

Imagine that . . . Job prayed for those who had actually made things worse for him. But Job felt for (and with) his friends in the face of God's rebuke of them—and the suffering that he knew that these friends would now face. In this moment of the story, Job actually joined the others in empathy. Perhaps they joined Job, as well. They came together for the first time in a *shared witness* to suffering. In this pivotal moment, they became an empathetic community of mutual care. Examined in that way, the story shifts from punishment and retribution to Love.

Another, potentially even better take-away is this: God didn't reinstitute Job's losses in the end. God didn't make things all go back to the way they were. Now God *did* restore Job's fortunes. Two-fold, in fact. And restored his health. Job's family and friends came to visit and celebrate with Job and his wife. But Job didn't get his children back. They had perished, and they weren't returning. So Job and his wife would always mourn their loss of loved ones so dear to them. It's possible that the Bible doesn't give enough attention to this continued loss in Job's life. But, according to the story, God did restore children to them. New children. Many new children. Not the same ones, though. Not a return of something lost. Instead, a transformation in the face of loss. It implies going forward in a different way. Joyful, but different nonetheless.

Perhaps the greatest take-away of the story is this, though: that God did not curse Job in the face of Job's heart-felt queries. Job questioned God in a passionate, earnest way in order to discover some degree of truth in his suffering. Job was clearly angry, overwhelmed, frustrated, frightened, and disillusioned. But he didn't give up on God. In fact, Job refused to be drawn into simple, but erroneous, 'untruths' that his own guilt and sinfulness were the causes of his suffering from God. For the story tells us at the outset that Job was righteous. So even if you accept the dubious belief system that bad people have bad stuff coming to them by God, Job didn't deserve any of it. Not one bit.

In the face of this injustice, Job had every reason to walk away from God. But he didn't. He didn't shut himself down. To be fair, Job *did* back away toward the end, according to the story. But he certainly didn't walk away. For in the face of not receiving any plausible explanation from God, Job turned toward his now-cursed friends. And he prayed for them. He got outside of his own notions of 'truth' and he reached out to others beside him. Equally importantly, God didn't shut down either. God never told Job to 'shut up'. God didn't demand that Job back down and get out of God's face. In fact, God 'answered' Job's questions with other questions. Perhaps God was telling Job that, in reality, the answers actually reside in God's questions themselves.

The only people who shut down were Job's friends. The very friends who came to visit Job in order to comfort him in the first place. In truth, they didn't actually comfort Job at all. But they *did* shut themselves down. They did so precisely because they couldn't stop talking. Because they couldn't stop their own moralizing. Because they couldn't resist drawing on all of the standard lines of the day. In effect then, however unintentionally, *they* shut themselves and Job down. Or at least tried to.

So, while Job's friends shut themselves out, neither Job nor God shut down the quest for truths. The notion that God doesn't want our questions about what is 'true', no matter how difficult the questions might be, is *our* notion. Not God's. So we often shut ourselves down in our own lives. Sometimes we give up way too easily. Because we're afraid that we'll disrespect God. Or that we'll make God angry in the process. Or become a pest. In our quest for truths. But however counter-intuitive it may seem, we serve the quest for truths *best* when we *never* shut down . . .

. . . When we never shut down our willingness to live more readily with the questions. The many questions that inherently define the notion of actual living. And the questions that surround any human idea of truths. For life and truths, themselves, are both embedded with questions. We go wrong when we seek 'the' answers to life's 'truth' mysteries. Instead of seeking peace in the questions. Instead of remaining humbly open to what we simply can't know as humans.

We should embrace this limitation instead of fretting about it. Or pretending that we can know what is ultimately true—until we can't do so any longer in a crisis. In this regard, it's not that only God knows all things and that we can never know certain things. It's not that God is withholding stuff about truth from us in our lives. That would be a test. Just like the test that we, all too often, think God was dumping on Job in the Bible. I don't believe it was a test at all. Not then. Not now. Not for Job. Nor for us.

Further, we're not being graded on how well we do in the face of ambiguity. It's not about finding out the best or only answer from God. Or trying to coax an explanation for everything from God. Rather, it's that living life *is* 'living the questions' in many ways. The question *is* the answer. We don't grow as spiritual people by passing a test. Because it isn't a test at all. But we *do* stretch ourselves in our quest for truths by getting better at asking the right questions. Then being at peace with them. That's worth an A+.

On 'Truly' Being

The line between true greatness and true dullness of 'being' is thinner and more porous than we might think. The separation of 'either' and 'or' is also often blurred amidst the chaos, randomness, and centrifugal forces that act on us continuously. Further, we operate in a world populated by many others, who influence us in so many ways. We live and work in societies, groups, and organizations that exert powerful, if sometimes subtle, pressure on us to conform, to believe, and to follow. Our apparent choices may, therefore, be false ones. With limited built-in, prearranged parameters and options laid out for us. Human 'being' in all its greatness is therefore difficult. So is reaching our true destination . . . the quest for truths borne in our very hearts . . . deep within our very souls.

In the midst of this all, here is the question to consider: will we embark on the quest for truths knowing that, ironically enough, *the way there is* the actual destination? If our answer is yes, our reasons for embracing the quest are likely to change en-route. For, in truth, things may never be entirely clear. We may never know that which lies just ahead of us. We understand imperfectly and only in part. We swim upstream amidst a turbulent current. Others will, most certainly, try to pull us beneath the surface. We may even feel like we're gasping for air at times. We'll face darkness. We'll hit headwinds. We'll meet struggle and resistance. We'll sleep with the mystery of it all. We'll slog through doubt. But, if the quest for truths is truly worth it, then so is the journey itself.

As we seek truths, many of us turn to 'religion' for support. For some, our religion is our faith. For others, our religion is our science. And, for others, it is our belief systems. We may find religion in our belongings. Or in our passions. In our worldviews. Our political parties. Our positions on issues. Our causes. Our projects. Even our jobs. However constituted, our religions create stories and myths to ease our existential anxiety.

This anxiety is grounded in the inherently and chaotically 'unknowable' aspects of our planet, creation, life, suffering, death, and our hoped-for immortality. Our 'religions' can be helpful in easing our anxieties and allowing us to function each day in an admittedly scary world. Further, these religions can, admittedly, provide a sense of abiding human hope. But, conversely, they can *also* be harmful when they claim to hold the 'sole truth'. About anything at all. This supposition is valid for many reasons. But there's one in particular that's worth exploring here.

For when we claim exclusive truth, we actively embrace an agenda. As previously mentioned, we often do so in order to ease our understandable uncertainties and our fears. But we also embrace a potential 'truth' in order to control our destinies. To set us apart from others. To belong to something. To fit into a group. To adhere to established, predictable norms. To believe in something specific and 'knowable'. Sometimes, we incorporate an absolute truth to win at the expense of others. Winners and losers. To be on the right side. The winning side. To get the prize. The grand prize.

It's enticing, to be sure. Because when we append exclusive truth to ourselves, we feel invincible. Redeemed. Special. Different. But here's the problem: the very act of appending truth is, in truth, an act of personal and spiritual disempowerment . . . and of losing. Because when we do so, the appended truth of another person or institution actually feels like our truth. But it's really someone else's. We've become part of someone else's dream. Another's view of reality.

And, as a result, our own dream has now been co-opted by the other. We've joined the powerful, magnetic cartel of *their* belief. Their system of being. Their norms. Their expectations. Their community. And their system works hard to keep us firmly entrenched. Fully entrenched. Encapsulated. In their box. In their dream. But so tragically in the process, we've become lost in *our own* unanticipated nightmare of disjointed, fragmented 'non-being' in the end.

Given this, what if our deliverance and redemption from 'non-being' can be better achieved in another way? By purposefully avoiding our human need for attachment to absolutes in life. By remaining open and curious. By accepting and embracing uncertainty and diversity. It can actually work because truths reside in the nuanced, complex recesses of the concentric circles of our beings. Both as individuals and as members of groups in society. And God probably speaks to us in different ways, anyway. How God 'speaks' to you may be different that how God 'speaks' to me.

In this regard, I propose that we can live, learn, and quest more meaningfully toward truths *only* by also listening to the stories of God's words to others, not just ourselves. Yes, even other peoples. Other religions. Other societies. Other regions. Other times. Other contexts. What's more, God most likely calls us not to a single 'truth'. Rather, we're called to a continuous journey of seeking truths wherever they may be found. In fact, the only ultimate, sacred truth may be this: *we need to continuously seek truths and that of God within each of us, respectively.*

If this is the case, our human quest rests not on belief at all. Not on 'truth'. Instead, it's grounded firmly in building our capacity for growth as spiritual human beings. Grounded in our capacity to resist dogmatic, rigid, exclusive 'truth'. And in our dogged determination to stretch inclusively beyond our respective comfort zones. To change and transform. To take and make meaning from all things sacred. To embrace possibility over certainty. To live richly in this moment, not in the past or the future. To open ourselves and our hearts to new ideas with curious ears and eyes. To join with each other in loving communion.

And, in the process, to unbind and to 'become' . . . to fully and truly 'be'. Truth. Word.

Out-of-the-Box . . . for a Change

Go ahead and admit it, we've all heard this said many times. "Paint by the numbers. Color within the lines. Play in the middle of the field. Between the hash marks, preferably. Play it safe. Keep safe. Stay safe. Stay 'true' to yourself. With your feet planted firmly and squarely on the ground. Or more specifically in the box." If we're honest, most of us have lived our lives that way. Safely and cautiously inside the box. And we've learned the lesson well. To be fair here, it sometimes takes courage and fortitude to stay there. Particularly when we're facing intense pressure to cut corners. To fudge the rules. To get the upper hand. To unfairly get what's 'ours'. Or to win at all costs.

But, more often than not, it takes *far more* courage to let go of a 'sure thing', the cautious and safe thing, and to move outside the lines. To push ourselves to transcend what's already been laid out before us. To challenge accepted notions of truth, rules, patterns, and relationships. Then take a risk. And perceive the world around us in new ways. To try connecting the seemingly unrelated. To act in different, new ways in order to seize possibilities. To forgo certainty in the service of courageous hope and promise.

When we do, we're sure to face the judgments of our families, friends, and peers. We'll be criticized as dreamers, utopians, and idealists. We'll feel the constant tug of past emotional comforts on us. They're like the soothing balm of a juice box, a blanket, and a large bowl of chicken soup. Perhaps we'll be more scared than ever before in our entire lives. We'll risk feeling alienated, pessimistic at times, and downright doubtful on some days. We'll feel the hard pull of linear, incremental thinking. We'll hear the countless voices of those who tell us, "This will never work. It's been tried before and it failed. Just give it up and come back to reality." Or "This is nuts. Play by the rules, buddy. Get back in the game of life. Stop your dreaming!" Or "This just can't be true. You're living in a delusional state of mind, my friend."

So being unique and different in a herd is hard. Swimming against the current is really hard. Trekking the way less traveled is excruciatingly difficult. Thinking and living outside the 'accepted truth box' is truly big. No denying that. But it doesn't require a giant leap at the outset. Instead, we can do many *little* things each day to incrementally foster our creativity and to grow our courage. Sometimes simply changing our venue can help to sort out a problem. In other words, take the problem or search for truths to a new location. Change things up. You might look at the issue differently in a park than you would on a busy street. Or in a coffee shop instead of in your own living room at home.

Next, try looking at a problem or accepted notion from another's viewpoint. I don't mean asking other people what they'd do or what they think. For they'll probably just reinforce your reticence to be more creative in the first place. They're likely to pull you right back into your current trap of normalcy and the status quo. So rather than that, try taking time to learn about other, more creative icons in history. Then ask yourself, aloud, how these people might have thought about the issue at hand? Learn how others have addressed something broadly similar, but in dissimilar ways in the past. Be inspired by others who've gone against the grain in history or in current times. Study the behaviors and lives of creative, challenging people.

Part of breaking out-of-the-box also entails asking different questions about your challenge. Instead of fixating on the need to immediately resolve the problem or find the 'right way', step back for a moment. Start from your basic wants, needs, and objectives for a change. If you're clearer on what you're ultimately trying to achieve, you can more effectively think through creative alternatives to address those longer-term needs. In the process of this needs based thinking, separate your short-term from your longer-term needs. Too often, we focus only on the short-term. In the process, we hinder the 'longer-term' to our long-term detriment. We may have to sacrifice something now to get to where we ultimately want to be down the road.

In the final analysis, thinking outside-the-box is a spiritual truths seeking exercise. For it involves our digging more deeply into our souls. It takes enormous courage to see something not just from the perspective of its outward, external symptoms. For, in truth, it's far easier to simply address the symptoms. To put a Band-Aid on things and to stop the bleeding now. But the symptoms often merely mask the more important causes underneath. Symptoms are just that. They're the universe's way of telling us that something is fundamentally wrong inside. Internal pain is nature's warning sign to us if we're willing to open our eyes, hearts, and minds.

This kind of opening happens *only* when we think differently than we've ever done before. Awakening unfolds when we seek out new people and different perspectives in our lives. It occurs when we're willing to openly brainstorm with objectively thinking 'others' with a less critical and possessive lens. With others who don't harbor their own agendas already set in stone. It occurs when we're willing to truly listen to *every* idea for a change. Someone else's idea may not be the best one in the end. But it might allow you to build on it in a novel, creative way. Or to take part of it and to incorporate that component of 'truth' into a more logical, holistic solution for you. In this way, creative input is a stepping-stone to another idea. Then another. And then to something amazing and creative in the end.

Thinking outside-the-box may be the hardest thing you've ever had to do. But it is worth it if you stay at it. When you periodically feel discouraged and resisted in your endeavor, try not to dwell only on the hoped for solution or the problem to be solved. No. 'Think' outside the lines even here. *Stop thinking for a moment. And start feeling.* Take time to 'wonder within' about how you'll actually feel when the problem is successfully behind you. When you've landed on the right approach for you. And don't focus on the relief that you'll undoubtedly feel now that the challenge has been met. Instead, wonder how you'll actually be different and changed and truer and better as a human being as a result.

This is the crux of living more creatively. Problems and challenges will constantly come and go in our lives. We can be certain of that. But we're far better able to handle them when we've learned to paint without the numbers. When we've learned to step appropriately outside the hash marks of the playing field at times. And to color outside the lines. To even ditch the actual coloring book for once. To lock it away in a box somewhere. And work creatively from a clean sheet of paper for a change. That's transformative. In a truly Out-Of-The-Box kind of way.

Guess Who's Coming To Dinner

The groundbreaking 1967 film, *Guess Who's Coming to Dinner*, courageously confronted the highly sensitive issue of interracial marriage. Interracial marriage had been historically banned in the United States, and restrictions were still in place in many states at the time. The U.S. Supreme Court struck down all state anti-miscegenation laws that same year in the case of <u>Loving v. Virginia</u> on the grounds that these restrictive laws violated the Constitution. In a spiritual sense, the Court held that interracial marriage was one *basic truth* of inclusive human fellowship.

The 2nd Testament Gospels of the Bible spend a fair amount of space in discussing this inclusive fellowship truth. But in a different way. And it's often in the context of stories regarding food. We read about Jesus feeding the multitudes. About his sharing bread and wine with his disciples as a sign of his blessing. Christ's miracle of turning water into wine at the wedding in Cana. Even his highly unsettling revelation to the Jewish crowds in the Gospel of John. In this story, Jesus proclaimed to the people, "Amen, amen I say to you, unless you eat the flesh of the Son of Man and drink his blood, you do not have life within you . . . For my flesh is true food and my blood is true drink."

Given the multitude of Gospel stories in this area, it's fair to say that table fellowship and food weren't simply 'events'. They were integral to the broader truth of Jesus. But the Biblical crowds who recoiled at Christ's references to eating and drinking his flesh and blood may have entirely missed the point. For they were fixated on their existing notions of clean and unclean dietary restrictions and laws. And, understandably, they were unnerved by the notion of possible cannibalism. So, in this story, the crowd jumped to argumentative, resistant conclusions about Christ's teaching on consuming his flesh and blood.

The crowd's focus (and resultant misinterpretation) were driven by commonly accepted, existing notions of eating as an important part of their religious practices. In fact, sharing table fellowship was a crucial aspect of life in ancient societies of the time. Things like appropriate invitees, status-based seating locations, food selection, and etiquette all mattered greatly. These were tangible, literal, and specific *signs* of cultural and religious practices and protocol.

But Jesus didn't follow the norms and 'truths' of the times in many ways. Jesus invited those shunned by 'acceptable society' to the dinner table. He was inclusive and regularly used table fellowship as a way to share, teach, celebrate, and challenge existing practices. It was an integral part of his ministry. In fact, some detractors argued that Jesus was a glutton and a drunk because of his practices.

But they got it wrong. And, sadly, so do we at times. For Christ's table fellowship was, and is, about *the meal as a metaphor of truth*. A metaphor of true, divine hospitality. A new social order. A new notion of human community. About breaking down barriers. About relaxing hurtful barriers, protocols, and perceived rigid 'truths' that only separate us in the end. About creating a mutually interdependent, healing, connecting experience instead. But we miss the metaphor when we get hung up on the meal itself. And when we fixate on 'flesh and blood' in strictly spiritual, religious terms.

To illustrate, we use 'flesh and blood' a lot in our worship practices and beliefs. These words get thrown around in the context of sinfulness, sacrifice, ritual, and sacrament. Perhaps some of it is justified based on Biblical interpretation. But we get in trouble when we overlook the core functions that 'flesh' and 'blood' connote in our very lives. For our *flesh* is part of our human musculoskeletal system—providing our very form and physique; allowing our movement; protecting our internal organs; storing nutrients; binding our bones in place; and keeping us stable and connected. Our *blood* is our very life source. It carries oxygen, nutrients, and immunity-protective substances to our cells. As such, our flesh and our blood aren't simply life sustaining for us. These terms also imply an integrative, connecting, and mutually interdependent bodily fellowship *within* us.

As such, it's possible that we 'miss the plot entirely' when we lose this 'fleshly' analogy of our human bodies. Further, when we narrowly fixate on Christ's body and blood as our means of salvation, we can too easily lose a critical thread of the truth of Jesus. We can overlook Christ's own regular practice of divine table fellowship and sharing. And his potential reference to his own 'body and blood' as a truth metaphor for our interdependent, shared functioning as human beings.

Christ used the symbols of flesh and blood to make a crucial point. And not just one about individual salvation though him. No. His message was far deeper than that. In the Biblical story, Jesus spoke out to the crowds (and, by extension, to us) in order to actually challenge them and us. However provocatively and uncomfortably it might seem on the surface. He stood before them to invite them (and, by extension, *each* of us) to the table, as it were. An invitation to a new, truer human order. A new inclusive fellowship of true togetherness. So guess who's coming to dinner tonight. Who are you inviting? And will Jesus be there, at the table, in spirit?

Our Quest for Truths

'Quest'-ions for Prayer and Further Reflection

- In what ways do you tend to 'miss the forest for the trees' in taking what you learn, read, and hear too rigidly and literally?
- How often have you stuck with what you already think you know or believe to your possible detriment? Why? And with what results?
- How much of your faith is currently driven by your specific needs, wants, fears, self-judgment, guilt, or felt-need for rigid obedience? What do you think drives this?
- How helpful and supportive has your own 'truth' been when you are faced with serious setbacks, disappointments, losses, or suffering?
- How might you open yourself more fully to God's free-flowing, spontaneous, even playful, childlike love through the Spirit?

Our Quest for Things Sacred

Sacred:

- *Something worshipped, venerated, or fervently devoted to*
- *A divine, holy thing or person*
- *Secured against disrespect, violation, harm, or irreverence*
- *Entitled to deep respect by human beings*
- *Valued and sought after as vitally important*

Burning the Bridges Behind You

THE POPULAR PHRASE '*Not in my Backyard*' (NIMBY) refers to our human tendency to oppose locating something or someone deemed undesirable or of questionable value in our own neighborhoods. It's meant to head-off the prospect of a thing or a person perceived as unwanted, unsightly, harmful or dangerous, deleterious of property values, or a source of anticipated pollution. It's often applied to proposals in communities for jails, refuse dumps, public housing projects, rehabilitation centers, homeless shelters, halfway houses, or 'dirty' industries.

It's based, at least in part, on our feelings of 'sacred' entitlement. Our sense that we're 'elevated' and far better than the thing or the group of people that we oppose or resist. That we're somehow purer than others. And that we shouldn't be 'corrupted' by messy, unclean outside interlopers. Must not be infused or mixed with people or with things beneath our current station in life. More often than not, wild speculation, discrimination, and copious amounts of unwarranted *fear and loathing* fuel this opposition.

Our Quest for Things Sacred

In the Biblical 2nd Testament Gospel of Matthew, Jesus assures his disciples that the day is coming when the malice, wickedness, and hypocrisy of those who falsely proclaim faith in God will be revealed. God's truth will be ultimately proclaimed and victorious in the Kingdom of God. But this Kingdom promise is viscerally juxtaposed with the polar opposite extreme: Gehenna, a place of God's eternal judgment, damnation, and punishment of both bodies and souls of offenders.

As Christians, we're taught that Jesus offers his Biblical 'Kingdom words' to his disciples in the form of both an encouragement and a warning. Christ's message is meant to encourage the disciples' strength and fortitude in the face of almost certain fear, persecution, and even future death in proclaiming God's truth to their many powerful adversaries. Conversely, the words serve as a foreboding, fearful warning for those who deny God in practice, no matter how sanctimonious they might outwardly seem. A warning to those who don't actually 'walk the talk'.

Historically (and Biblically) speaking, Gehenna was a ravine located south of Jerusalem in Biblical times. It was located in the Valley of Hinnon. This place was 'outside the walls' of accepted ancient Jewish society in every sense of the word. It was initially referenced in the Bible's 1st Testament book of Joshua, as part of the setting of boundaries of the territory of Judah. In other words, what's within, and by extension, without the territorial lines.

This notable ravine took on darker characteristics in 2 Chronicles when King Ahaz sacrificed children to false gods there. The prophet Jeremiah subsequently called Hinnon the 'Valley of Slaughter', where corpses of people became food for animals of prey. Prey that were never frightened away. In the Biblical story, Jeremiah was instructed by God to prophesy God's coming judgment against those who shed innocent blood in the name of idolatry. God told Jeremiah to shatter a piece of pottery before his audience to make God's point visually. For they, too, would be shattered if their evil ways continued.

So Gehenna (and the Valley of Hinnon) take on frightening dimensions for Bible readers. It was a place of suffering, death, abominable human sacrifice, and judgment. It was literally and figuratively a place of rejection, removal, and separation 'outside the walls' of society and faith communities. The valley was also a place where criminals were buried in these times. Garbage was burned here, as well. The fires burned constantly, as there was a never-ending supply of refuge to be incinerated. The idea of 'Not in my

Backyard' would have certainly applied . . . fueled by copious amounts of fear.

How fitting, then, that Jesus' warning in the Gospel of Matthew also accentuates the notion of rejection with the image of a Sparrow. The sparrow is a small bird. It was found in great numbers in Biblical times in this geographic area. The Bible tells us that sparrows were worth very little in monetary value. Most perceived them as troublesome, intruding birds. Sparrows constantly foraged for food like grain, seeds, and insects. While sometimes solitary and alone, they could also fly in large clusters. People of this place and time would have gladly banished these pesky birds to another place. The idea of 'Not in my Backyard' would have certainly applied . . . fueled by copious amounts of loathing.

Here's the problem with all of this: we too often read Christ's words of warning to his disciples (and to the crowds of followers around him) as his sacred 'heads up' surrounding God's coming judgment. To comfort believers and to truly warn those who had fallen away. But we may miss the point entirely if we fail to see things more holistically in the broader sense of rejection. Not just God's but ours as well. For when we cry out 'Not in my Backyard' to others, we reject them. We exclude them. We might even try to physically remove and banish them. Like trash, 'criminal' elements, or even dead sparrows to the waste heaps of Gehenna. And not just remove them, but to sit in our own unsacred sanctimonious judgment of them in the process.

But there's more. Many Biblical scholars argue that Gehenna wasn't just a place of destruction. It was also a place of eternal punishment, torment, and judgment. By extension, when we throw others out of our own 'sacred' cities, sanctuaries, and walls into our own modern day version of Gehenna, we don't simply destroy them. Instead, we also judge them, somehow believing that they actually deserve their punishment. That they need to truly feel the pain. So we keep on punishing them through our exclusion and marginalization. And the suffering perpetuates itself in perpetuity. Like brick after brick on the pile of rejection. 'Not in my Backyard' with copious amounts of fear, loathing, and irrational beliefs about how we're solely entitled to the mantle of sacredness.

But what if we looked at Jesus' Biblical words from a different angle for a change? Perhaps Jesus wasn't telling his disciples to persevere in the face of almost certain persecution for belief in him. He *may* have been warning them against the tyranny of feeling 'included and entitled' in some inner sacred sanctum. He may have admonished them that those on the inside can start feeling superior and self-sanctimonious. That, if they're not careful, they can unwittingly build very unsacred walls of separation between themselves and the outside 'undesirables'. And that, in the process, begin to look down in distain on the little sparrows of this world. And hold themselves out as somehow better in nature.

Here's the thing. Jesus knew better and still does. For when we reject others and consign them to the trash heaps of 'Gehenna' outside the walls, we judge *ourselves*. Ironically enough, it's not the 'unworthy' outsiders who burn in eternal suffering. No. It's actually *us* who begin to burn up on the inside. It's *we* who actually destruct and self-incinerate as we wait for the fires to start on the outside. We end up judging ourselves as unworthy—even as we try to judge others in that vein. Therefore, we need to be very careful when we raise the rally cry of 'Not in my Backyard'. Because the line between who's in and who's out of the 'sacred club' is thinner and more blurred than we might otherwise believe.

The 'Ark' of the Covenant

The Biblical story of Noah's Ark parallels those of many other ancient flood mythologies and narratives. While these different stories varied in some important respects, most of them encompassed some elements of extinction, survival, and the human quest for a measure of immortality. More broadly, they captured ideas of the creation, destruction, redemption, and renewal of something truly sacred. A replanting of what was flooded out or destroyed. The floods were caused by God's judgment of our human sinfulness or via the caprice or mischief of 'gods', depending on the story's respective sources.

In the 1st Testament Biblical account of the floods, escape entailed the building of a floating vessel or an Ark—using the boat to save a sacred remnant of life for the replanting of the 'seed' after the floods had subsided. As part of this story, God also made a sacred covenant with Noah and his family, the only humans to escape the raging waters. God blessed Noah, calling him to be fruitful and multiply. God gave the earth's creatures and living things into Noah's hands to be a steward for the future. Further, God promised to never again flood the earth, sealing this covenant with a rainbow in the sky.

The parallels of all these ancient flood stories to our own current situation are frightening and striking indeed. We need only gaze out into the world right now. Or read a bit. 'Engage' with what our sacred planet is trying to urgently tell us. Our waters and seas are rising. Glacial melt and higher temperatures threaten our coastlines. Storms are becoming more deadly. Animal and plant species are disappearing at alarming rates. We're witnessing greater extremes in temperatures. Draughts and floods abound. Wildfires burn with increased regularity, charring and scorching the soil. Experts are warning that portions of our globe will become entirely uninhabitable before the end of the 21st Century because of climate change.

But there's no shortage of skeptics and deniers. Like those who mocked and criticized Noah for building the Ark, far too many have mockingly turned their eyes and their backs on the unmistakable environmental reality that now confronts us. Rather than investing in proactive ways to save our planet, we're trying to figure out ways to reverse the ongoing damage to it. While continuing to pollute our world. To further complicate things, we're making matters even worse. For example, we're cutting down the very trees that effectively absorb the deadly carbon gas that we've recklessly spewed into the skies. Further, rather than multiplying 'fruitfully' in responsible ways, we're ignoring the incapacity of this planet to sustain unmanageable population growth over an extended period of time.

Others among us simply dream about getting away from it all. We're beginning to muse about travel to Mars. Perhaps we'll even colonize the Red Planet one day. Then escape the mess we've created right here at home on Earth. Just fly away. And subjugate another planet. But here's the thing. It's a bankrupt plan. It's unrealistic. It's shameful. Merrily destroying (then leaving behind) our sacred planet earth is bereft of any conscience and soul. For when we do it, we utterly and completely forsake God's call to us to be responsible stewards. Stewards and protectors of life right here. Sacred life that God has gifted us to care for and nurture.

So what's the outgrowth of this all? God creates. Then we destroy our life-source with an arrogant hubris. As if we're greater than God's promise *to never again* destroy the earth in the Biblical story of Noah. We can try to deny, deflect, obfuscate, criticize, mock, blame, and hide the facts all we want. We can hope for some dramatic rescue by the 'tooth fairy'. We can pretend to look the other way as the waters rise. But it doesn't change the reality before us. The story of our planet is unmistakably speaking to us. Just like the sacred flood narratives of the past.

When we read the Biblical story of Noah, it's easy to see it only as 'history' or some allegorical story about the past. Then to dismiss it as irrelevant to today's world. But think outside-the-box here. What if Noah's Ark and other stories like it aren't really histories at all? Not about looking back. Instead, these epics might *most* appropriately stand as *precautionary* tales. *Prophetic predictions* from the past to us now. About the coming, dreadful fate that awaits us all if we don't heed the warnings. Or if we continue to hold the 'prophets' in scorn. Just like the crowds did to Noah as he built the Ark.

Perhaps, then, the moral of the Biblical Noah story is this: if we continue on our current path, we'll all be wiped out. Destroyed. Flooded. And drowned. Further, like the account of Noah and the Ark, only a small remnant will remain. For an Ark can carry only so many people. Only so many animals. Only so many plants. Actually not many, to be honest. Nearly all will be left behind. Or more specifically, left for 'gone'. Washed up . . . literally.

Rather than merely preaching doom here, there's another way: the Way of the Rainbow. In the story of Noah, God promised to never again flood and destroy the earth. And God sealed this promise with a rainbow. Which one of us hasn't marveled at the majesty and sheer beauty of a rainbow in the sky? Its many diverse colors are inclusively splashed and stretched from one horizon to the other. It is breathtaking and undeniably hopeful. The colors and breadth of the rainbow's arc remind us that saving our planet will take *all of us*. Everyone. From every place and every horizon. To come together and mesh inclusively in this most pressing, sacred cause. To solve this and save ourselves. In so doing, to *become* the rainbow rather than flying over it as we try to escape the carnage that we've created.

But if we're going to actually be the rainbow, we need Light. The good news in this regard is that God has placed the light that we need within us *already*. And it's time to turn these lights on. Perhaps we've already reached the tipping point and it's too late to illuminate the sky. I'd rather think otherwise. So let's light the rainbow right now with some real urgency. Let's forget about the Ark and sign the Covenant. As caring, responsible, loving stewards of our sacred planet earth. Before the rainbow goes dark forever and sinks eternally into the rising flood.

'Above' the Iceberg

Sometimes icebergs just float around out there in the cold waters of the ocean. All by themselves. Cut away from the ice shelf from which they have calved and broken off. What we actually see, however, is only what lies *at* the water's surface. No matter how large or small, tall or short the iceberg, we view only part of it. And the part that we see is often blue, as the denseness of the ice blocks out all other colors in the spectrum.

In today's world, many of us are like loose, floating icebergs. Stories abound of people who have left their 'homes'. Like calving ice sheets. Then have literally floated away alone. We move from our neighborhoods of origin. From our families of origin. Sometimes across the entire country. Or to another country. We move for new jobs, for pleasure, for warmer weather, or for cheaper real estate. We move for lower taxes, better healthcare, safer surroundings, friendlier neighbors, or lower stress. Increasingly, Baby Boomers are migrating to burgeoning 'active adult' communities. To find comfort and friendship in places where other seniors live. To find 'community' with like-minded and similarly aged grown-ups. We seek out those people we deem similar to ourselves. Those who are more like us. In 'like' conclaves and clans.

Seeking things that are just like us is nothing new. In the 1st Testament of the Bible, God called for God's people to go to the Promised Land. To find and settle the place that God had given into their hands. We read that God also commanded God's people to destroy the idolatrous inhabitants already living there. To totally refrain from inter-marrying with them. To remain fully apart from their influences. However, we also learn that God's people didn't always do that—in direct contradiction to God's supposed commands. Notwithstanding evidence that settlement of the Promised Land was gradual and incremental (not done with a 'clang and bang' crossing the Jordan River), God's people assimilated with those already there to at least some extent.

Lest we blame the subsequent split and downfall of the Kingdoms of Israel and Judah on this failure to annihilate the enemy, it's important to note the following: the ultimate invasion of the Promised Land and the exile of God's people were grounded in internal division and strife, not outside forces. As such, the problem was far less about those who were 'different'. Far more about those who were the 'same'. So in the end, striving for 'like me' purity didn't work out in the 1st Testament Bible. It still doesn't work today. Because 'like me' unnecessarily separates and divides us from each other.

Let's explore our human divisions by returning to the idea of an iceberg on the ocean. For purposes of this illustration, pretend that we're all icebergs for a moment. On the water's surface, icebergs vary by size, height, breadth, width, and configuration. As people, we also vary on the 'surface'. By this I mean the things that we can readily see about each other or can easily learn by asking a few questions. While we're all people on the surface, we're different. Richly so. We vary by our race and ethnicity. According to our gender. Our age. Our religious affiliation. Our socio-economic status. Our town or city. Our country of residence. The language that we speak. Our sexual orientation or identity. To name just a few.

To more fully comprehend our differences as people, we need to go beneath the water's surface. For, *below our surfaces* as human 'icebergs', we see far more sacred and spiritual differences. We differ by our life's experiences and life's stories. By our respective values. By those things that give meaning and purpose to us as human beings. Further, we come from different heritages. We also carry different perspectives, belief systems, and world-views. Our education varies by level, type, context, and specialties. Our ways of relating to others in the world also vary tremendously. Our skills are different. As are the ways in which we observe, learn, and integrate knowledge.

We're different in so many varied and sacred ways. If only we'll take time to look *under* the water's surface. And these differences add richness to our lives. For we learn best from our differences, not from our similarities. In fact, inclusion is just that: trying to understand our differences in an open, welcoming way. Honestly exploring and acknowledging our biases, whether conscious or unconscious. Then doing our best to overcome these biases. And, therefore, welcoming the entire range of our differences as building blocks to a better, more spiritually welcoming sacred world.

However, the problem lies in our inability (or unwillingness) to do so in many cases. We can't get past our comfort zones of hanging out with those who look, act, and believe just like we do. The 'similar-to-me' effect is powerful, indeed. It can easily resist our best efforts to stretch ourselves. It impacts our choices of jobs, of employees when we're hiring, of our mates, and of our friends. Oftentimes to our ultimate detriment and unhappiness. So how do we move past this solitary herding instinct as human beings? As with most things, change lies first within us.

When we become more centered, mindfully in the 'now', and comfortable in our own identities as loved human beings, it's easier to look outwardly in love and acceptance of others. Having better balance in our own lives helps, as well. If we're more balanced around meeting our mental, physical, spiritual, emotional, and interpersonal needs, we're more likely to take some personal risks spiritually. To stretch ourselves with people and things actually different than us. Differences at and directly below the surface of the proverbial waters around our respective personal icebergs.

Ironically enough, though, we must ultimately and inclusively encounter our differences not at the surface. Nor from underneath the water. But *from above*. We need to see ourselves as God sees us. This is the first and most important step. Because from above the surface, we're all human beings. We're all loved, sacred beings. Formed by God as special creatures, unique from other living species. Like all other living things, we are born and we'll die one day. We're mortal and finite in our earthly beings. But, as humans, our lives are far more nuanced and complex. For, perhaps unlike other creatures, we have the ability to seek and understand our place in the world. To be fully cognizant of our own mortality and to act in ways accordingly. We have the innate capacity to think beyond the immediate tasks at hand. To truly seek and find fulfillment and transcendence in our work and our sacred lives.

Furthermore, we have an innate desire to love and be loved. Not just romantically. But in a far greater, more far-reaching sense. We share this need. We mutually seek its fulfillment in our sacred beings. Finally, we share the desire for immortality. For some, this means going to Heaven after death. For others, it's about leaving a legacy behind. Whether an inheritance, children and grandchildren to carry on the family name, a lasting accomplishment or difference made, stories to hand down, or loving memories for the generations that follow our passing. We want and need to know that our lives have actually mattered.

So, in the end, there's much richness and value in all that lies at or beneath the 'water's surface' of our lives. But in order to think more deeply about ourselves, we need to get *above it all*. If we do, we'll most assuredly come to know this: no matter how diverse we appear to be, we all share the one thing that matters most. We share the lasting bond of common sacred humanity. And we begin, however haltingly but surely, to see all others in the way that God does. With love. Warm enough to melt the biggest iceberg out there.

Our Quest for Things Sacred

'Dislocated' Space . . . 'Found' Hope

The 2nd Testament contains the Christian Bible's final book: *Revelation*. This is, perhaps, the Bible's most misunderstood and confusing book. Revelation is often interpreted as a solely future-looking, end-of-time prophesy. But, in reality, it's more accurately seen as the Biblical author's admonishment and encouragement to the churches of that time. Specifically, the nascent Christian communities facing rampant, frightening, and violent persecution by the Roman Empire. The author may have been trying to lift the spirits and the fortitude of the understandably fearful believers.

It's as if the author wanted to assure everyone that things would be all right in the end. So that they wouldn't give up. Because God was near and was working in this space of fear and trembling. Amongst the most profound words of Revelation in this regard are these. "He will dwell with them as their God; they will be his peoples, and God himself will be with them; he will wipe every tear from their eyes. Death will be no more; mourning and crying and pain will be no more, for the first things have passed away."

It would be easy enough to take these radically profound and sacred words on face value. To see them simply as reassuring us that, in the end, God's plan and God's love will win. That God was working in history then. God continues to do so now. And God will do so in the future. God's got it covered. God's got the storybook ending already written. Further, it's tempting to remain and continuously abide in this message. For it's energizing, focusing, and comforting. But, tucked safely away in our homes, it is also too abstract. It seems antiseptic, distant, and far off. Because we're probably comfortable, warm, enclosed, and feeling relatively safe while reading.

So what if we 'got real'? You know, took this message to another place and reflected on it there? If we took our Bible and these Scriptural words in Revelation to a beautiful lake or stream or to an ocean nearby, the words might speak differently to us. For we'd be squarely in the midst of God's own physical creation—not in our respective homes. We might find the water calming, restorative, and relaxing. But sitting and gazing outward to the sea, we might ask ourselves this: I wonder what the New Heaven and the New Earth in this Bible passage of Revelation might look like?

It's an important question of context. For if there's no longer any sea, where will we swim and dip our toes? What will we drink to quench our thirst? Will we gaze upon nature's sacred splendor, as we know it now? Will there be other creatures in this new place? Or will it be just God and us? Will we be saddened to see the good things of this present earth pass away?

And how will the amazing, beautiful new earth be transported here? These are 'way-different' questions than we'd probably ask if we were reading the book's passage at home one evening in front of our fireplace.

Here's another twist. What if took the Revelation passage to our place of employment? Our job. In the midst of a crazy, hectic, highly stressful day. The Scripture's words might speak to us differently yet in this place. As we read it again, we'd probably wonder what kind of work might be undertaken in God's new creation. We might question why we expend so much of ourselves in our jobs anyway. We seem to give everything to these jobs, and we rarely have much energy left at the end of each day. We go home exhausted and burned out on a regular basis. Our jobs are important, to be sure. For they pay the bills and give us some measure of meaning. But the workplace can't be remotely as critical as other parts of our lives . . . parts that we may woefully neglect at the moment precisely because of our jobs.

If that's not enough, everything always seems so urgent in our work. It's always about 'now'. Always about getting the job done on time. We might wonder why there's not nearly as much urgency in our concern for our co-workers. We can get so busy with things that we often ignore others around us. We probably say "hello" to others each day. But we usually don't invest much of ourselves in our co-workers, to be honest. Why don't we focus more on each other? When we're hurting or crying. Or crying out for someone or anyone, really, to simply care. Why don't we see more clearly what God asks of us right here? In the office or workplace. Who will wipe away the tears of others if we don't take the time to do it for each other?

And yet another twist: what if we were to take this Revelation passage to a hospital and read it there as an inpatient? We might have any number of questions in response. Like where are you, God? Why is this disease or injury in my body? What is it doing to me? Who and where am I in all of this? Where are my support and my comfort? What happened to the things that once gave purpose and meaning to my life? They appear to have disappeared. Or thrown down, crumpled and torn on the hospital floor in the corner of my patient room. Why me, Lord? Why me?

Further, I wonder what I might pray about as I read the words of this passage in Revelation. While I lay in a hospital bed in the middle of the night. Alone. Exhausted. Or in pain. I might pray, "I am frightened, Lord. I've lost all control. I cry out . . . no I literally beg . . . for your healing and for a miracle. This new heaven and earth that you talk about in the Bible is fine, but I need a new 'me' now! Please make your new heaven and your new earth happen this instant in my body. You're all I have left, God."

So where we read this passage in Revelation really matters. Our respective contexts and locations always matter. It's easy to feel sanguine about God's sacred plan for us when we're safely snuggled up in our beds. When we feel safe. When we're not in pain. When we're ensconced in our tidy, warm homes. But when we take this passage out into the world, it raises questions. Lots of them. Sometimes these questions are interesting and even quizzical. Sometimes the questions radically challenge us. Then sometimes, the questions are existential and even painful. Like when our world or our body has completely crashed around us.

But, however challenging and difficult these questions may seem to us, we're given more in this Biblical passage of Revelation. For the book goes on to say this. "See, I am making all things new . . . It is done! I am the Alpha and the Omega, the beginning and the end. To the thirsty I will give water as a gift from the spring of the water of life. Those who conquer will inherit these things, and I will be their God and they will be my children." As such, no matter our location or the seeming dislocation in our lives, we can take heart. We can live with a measure of hope. Of expectancy. With positive intent. And assurance. And live life less anxiously. Because none of what befalls us has the last word on things.

For God is the beginning. And God is the end. We are of God and, therefore, transcend all time, all things, all pressures, all infirmities, and all fear. God's presence is a comfort and help. No matter where we're located. But this presence is also a sign: a sign of the coming new heaven and the new earth. Signs of God's sacred promises in this Biblical passage. In all times and in all places, we drink from God's future water in God's boundless well right now. Let there be peace in knowing that. Let there be assurance in God's *current* love—not just that love in the *future*. That love is both current and future, actually. And all tears will be wiped away. They will be dislocated. And, in their space, we'll find a greater sense of hope. Found, sacred hope.

Prayer as 'Reflexive'

The sun often casts shadows on a pond, lake, or a river. The images of trees and rocks that border the shore are projected onto the surfaces of the water along the banks. So, too, are the puffy clouds in the sky at times. They appear to literally sit on the water's surface as if transported through space onto the lake itself. As amazing as these reflections are, though, the images splashed on the water are not the things themselves. They're *projections* of the actual trees, rocks, and clouds– thanks to the sun and its many angles on the horizon. These images are vivid and clear when projected onto the calm water surface of a windless day. However, they become blurred when the waters churn in response to a heavy, sustained breeze.

Prayer is a lot like that, I suppose. We sometimes think that our prayers to God emanate completely from within ourselves. That *we're* the nexus and source of these prayers. And we believe that simply adding more words, more eloquent words, and somehow getting it 'right' will make our prayers even better in God's eyes and ears. In truth, though, our entire human prayer process can act in the same way as a steady wind on a lake. We can too easily forget that our prayers actually emanate in and from God, not by ourselves as we might think. Further, these prayers can become blurred by the windiness of our own speech and our own harried minds.

So what if we approached our prayers in a different way every so often? And set aside the formulaic algorithm that we so typically use. We know how it often goes in our prayers. We praise God. We thank God. We tell God what we need right now. We ask God for it. We thank God for it, in advance. Then we 'sign off'. Is that prayer? Or is it a monologue? Ours. Does it get us any closer to God? Or does it separate us further . . . by positioning God's love as conditional? Because if God hears us, God also needs to answer our prayers. God does this by giving us what we've asked for. Preferably as soon as possible.

And so it goes. God becomes a magician. Pulls another miracle out of the hat. God puts the toothpaste back in the tube. Gets the horse back into the barn. God becomes Santa God. Coming soon to a chimney near you to fill your wish list of needs. God dispenses favors like some mysterious cash machine at the bank. The First National Bank and Trust of God to be exact. Now there's nothing wrong with asking for God's favor, grace, and gifts. And there's nothing wrong with following a path of regular and specific prayer. But is that all there is here? What do we forsake and lose when we approach God with such strict and specifically needs-based prayer dialogue? Think about it. Are we praying *for* God or simply *to* God?

What would our approaching prayer differently actually look like? What if we simply sat with God in silence every now and then? Reverent silence. And listened to our breath. And imagined ourselves so close to and present with God that we were literally breathing God's outward breath as we take in that sacred air. Or what if we solely focused on a sacred image of God: such as a light, a heart, a lamb, an angel, or the idea of love? And let that image penetrate our very souls. Alternatively, what if we prayed with awe and wonder, simply musing on God as something and someone more amazing than *anything* that we've ever heard or read about? And what if our prayers focused far more on gratitude and thanks than on specific requests? Like spending an entire prayer each day on nothing but our expressions of gratitude to God.

Next, what if we simply 'spoke' silently in our mind to God one day? About nothing other than what we're going through and what we're feeling at that moment. Like sitting with and talking to a close friend. Simply asking God to engage with us in our troubles. God knows our troubles. But God wants us to share them anyway. God wants to hear our troubles, our doubts, our fears, and our hopes. Finally, what if we truly opened our hearts to prayer more holistically? And recognized that we *also* pray when we laugh, cry out, and shed tears. For those tears are not just our own. They are God's, as well. God's tears for us and truly with us. In the end, then, every component of our lives is prayer in a way. Not just what we typically call praying.

So, as we've seen, we're not the nexus of our lives or even our prayers. These things are of and from God, our creator and our friend. Our prayers are actually reflections of God's existent love, grace, and presence in our lives. In the same way that, as human living beings, we're really reflections of God's own creative genius and artistry. That said, praying to God goes beyond reflections, though. It goes far deeper still. For truly sacred prayer is *reflexive*, as well.

The word 'reflexive' is defined by one dictionary in this way: 'an act performed as a reflex, without overtly conscious thought.' Reflexive . . . What a concept. Applied to the act of praying, what if we approached our daily prayer more often in that light? And simply let it happen spontaneously without so much structure in our lives each day. You know, drop the script, the formulas, and even the words at times. Resist the abiding temptation to over-engineer our time of Godly fellowship. Instead, just sit with God for a change. And create an open, welcoming space for God to enter.

Some time ago, a family member of a patient that I had just seen as a hospital chaplain asked me a question following my visit and prayer. The patient's sister asked, "Why do we always bow our head and close our eyes when we pray together? It doesn't make any sense to me." Admittedly, the question caught me a bit off-guard in the moment. I've since reflected on it a good deal. But I still don't have a definitive answer that fully and spiritually satisfies me to be honest. So I continue to ponder.

The commonly accepted notion around that question is this: we bow our head and close our eyes in prayer to show reverence and respect. And to show humility before God as we pray. But let me take a counter-intuitive, contrarian approach here. If we're really reaching out to God and inviting God in through prayer, why not open our eyes? Why not lift our heads. Why not look at each other while praying together in a group. And take another person's hand. Then join *reflexively* in sacred and spontaneous prayer conversation, active listening, welcoming silence, and our tears. That would be reflexive for a change. Prayerfully so . . .

Sharing the Sacred Together

The world does not revolve around me. I live and breathe within it. All of it. Not just with living things. But with all things. Because I am rooted in the earth and in the soil. The sacred land. The land is life giving, life sustaining, life orienting, and life receiving in the end. It is a part of me. And 'I' of 'it'. When I begin to understand this, I see my own place in things more clearly. I can comprehend the enormity and complexity of everything around me. Things look bigger and more expansive. Everything seems more connected and joined up. I start to feel smaller in the midst of it all.

At first, that's a scary proposition in some ways. For it's easier when I think that I'm the 'King of the Heap'. The 'Queen of the Sand Pile'. The 'Grand Poopaah' of all things. The world is my platter. My snack tray. My juice bottle. My kingdom and castle. But when I let this go a bit and scale 'me' down, it actually lightens me up. Because I'm no longer responsible for everything. I'm not the lord of it all after all. Instead, I'm simply part of it all. What a relief.

As a result, my human spirituality means that I respect the sacredness of all creation. I live in harmony with it. Not with my boot on it. By extension, I live with reciprocity. This means that I try to restore what I remove. I'm careful about what I use. But when I need to use something, I try to make it whole somehow. And I say "thank you" to God for its use. I'm thankful because I have no inherent right to God's sacred creation. It's a gift. Freely given. But a gift nonetheless.

When I receive one of these gifts, I do so with humility and with gratitude. And I share the gift with others. Because community matters just as much as individuality. This means that creation is not 'dog eat dog'. Not even 'dog bite dog'. Not even a nibble. How about a kiss, instead? A kiss of interdependent, loving, caring, sharing mutuality. I share because it's the right thing to do. But also for this reason: I need others to share creation with me too.

God's sacred creation holds us together. We all belong to this place that we call earth, our home. And we also belong to each other. We were meant to breathe and talk and sing and cry and joyfully shout with others, not alone. And in a circle, actually. The earth is a sacred circle of sorts. So are we. The only way we can truly see each other is to stand in a circle. This means 'in the round'. Not on top of each other. Not in domination over others. Not from the rooftop overlooking others. But in a circle. A circle of life. A circle that allows us to see each other, to share with each other, and to lift each other when others are down.

A sacred circle that allows us to protect each other. So that we don't lose circle members. A circle that facilitates our loving one another. So that we don't let others down. This circle isn't a game of musical chairs. There are chairs for everyone. In a real circle. A big and diverse sacred circle. Woven out of the sacred earth itself. It's a circle where every chair, every person, and every living thing matters. All grounded in this place that we call home. Rooted firmly here and now. In the sacred earth. The sacred soil. The sacred ground. Rooted deeply.

'Quest'-ions for Prayer and Further Reflection

- In what ways do you attempt to 'possess' sacred things in your life? How does this negatively affect your judgment, decisions, actions, relationships, and your walk with God?
- How often do you simply ask 'for' God in your prayers, rather than asking for something of God? What are your real, underlying motivations in your prayers in this regard?
- How have you seen God working in our world creatively, wondrously, and spontaneously each day in God's sacred creation?

- How can you practice more solitude, meditation, and silence each day in better connecting with God's sacred presence around you?
- How can you be more 'contextual' in your spiritual listening and beliefs? How often do you really try to see the world through the eyes, situations, and lives of others, not simply your own?

Our Quest for Healing

Healing:

- *To be made well or healthy again*
- *To restore something or someone*
- *To ease or relieve pain, discomfort, and suffering*
- *To return to a state of integrity and wholeness*
- *To overcome something undesirable*

Solitary Confinement

EXPERTS HAVE INCREASINGLY SCRUTINIZED the debilitating physical, mental, and emotional affects of long periods of solitary confinement in our maximum-security prisons. 'Solitary' isn't a new concept—as its origins date back to the early 19th Century in the United States. Its genesis was the notion that individual holding cells and long periods of associated confinement would facilitate reflection, insights, and moral change by convicted inmates. As such, the motivation for 'Solitary' was initially far less about punishment than it was about rehabilitation.

Today, however, it's used far more in the former sense: for punishment. We employ solitary confinement in our prisons to protect the inmates or others from violence within institutions of incarceration. And we're hearing more stories from inmates and their families about the crushing and dehumanizing sense of isolation, depression, and even madness that sets in when prisoners are isolated over an extended period of time. It is truly cruel and unusual punishment for any individual to undergo. There's nothing remotely rehabilitating about it.

It's sadly ironic, then, that human beings often cloister *themselves* in 'Solitary' when they face losses, setbacks, sickness, or rejection by others. For many of us, our first instinct is to 'go to our rooms' in order to be alone when we're hurting. At times, it's just for a few hours. In other instances, however, our solitary confinement extends into days, weeks, or months. A time of reflection, introspection, and solitude can all too easily become a self-imposed solitary sentence. Far from a curative retreat, it can readily morph into entrenchment. Into spiritual decay and death.

In order to better understand our human tendency toward 'Solitary', we need to dig a bit deeper here. To what's underneath the concept. When we face life's inevitable crises, we often move from *'Object to Subject'*. This means that we feel entirely acted upon as a 'subject'. Something unfair is happening to us. Imposed on us. Afflicting us. At these times, it's terribly difficult to stand firm as 'object' in the crisis. For to be an object in this situation is to step back from it. In order to look at it somewhat more objectively and dispassionately. To try to understand it rather than by simply reacting to it. When the crush of trauma hits us, we're often sucked into the 'subject' place. And, in response, we seek out a quiet space. Away from it all. Away from others. Away, in turn, from ourselves in the process. Squarely in solitary confinement.

Entering into emotional 'Solitary' in response to crisis is like spending one's first few days in prison, I imagine. Our first human response is often *Survival*. We try simply to survive. Day-by-day. Hour-by-hour. Second-by-second. Our desire is solely to make it through the initial shock of things. So we sit in emotional and spiritual numbness for a while. We figuratively 'grow eyes in the back of our head' as we remain on-guard against the many menacing things around us. We might be spooked by sounds or voices. Or virtually anything or anyone for that matter.

To be fair, the 'sound' of silence is admittedly comforting in times of stress. We're lost in our thoughts, our sorrows, our pain, our anger, and our numbness. In a sense, though, survival is nothing more than mere 'existence'. Continuing to breathe while we disappear into a haze. Time begins to lose its meaning. Seconds move thoughtlessly into minutes and hours and days. The milestones of daily life fade slowly away. It probably feels comfortable, but our soul is also fading. Slowly away from us. Squarely in solitary confinement.

If we're brave enough to take a tentative step beyond Survival, we're likely to seek *Control*. Where surviving is all about continuing to exist, control is about making the painful parts go away. The figurative 'third eye' that we've grown behind our head now gets a pair of glasses. With extra thick lenses. The better to see with. We're likely to be defensive. To build a fortress around us. It might be a mattress or a desk or a couch. It might be a book or a TV or a game. These things are not distractions, though. They're actually walls and barriers that we're building around us. Like sleeping under the bed to hide from the monsters that lurk, however perceived or real.

The hallmark of control is finding a 'status quo'—preferably the 'quo' prior to the crisis itself. If that's not possible, sustaining a semblance of stability of one kind or another. Safety is paramount. Regaining a sense of homeostasis is the game. Our motivation is protection from further harm. A dug-in position, if you will. Trench warfare. On the defensive. From our bunker. It's as if we're trying to stop the world from circling. It's comforting to a degree.

For, if we can stop the world around us, we can try to make some sense of it. Spending some time in the control space isn't, therefore, all bad. Sometimes, we do need to dig-in for a while. But it's not a long-term strategy for human healing. For bunkers can suffocate us when we're entrenched too deeply. The air becomes stale and begins to run out. And it's just another form of solitary confinement. It's really a prison in disguise. Further, if we permit ourselves to see things more clearly, we'll realize how little we actually control things anyway. The world doesn't stop or even slow down, in spite of our best efforts or wishes. In fact, life goes merrily along around us even though we're anything but merry.

By coming to terms with this, we can tentatively take the next step: to actually get better. Wanting to make it better is a step, to be sure. It's movement in the direction of *Healing*. So it's a good thing in some respects. But we have to be careful even here. For making it better or making it heal can become a lot like our cries as a child to our parent when we fell down and hurt our knee: "Mommy, Mommy, make it go away!" Healing by only making it 'go away' is like taking an aspirin. Or swallowing an anti-inflammatory medicine. Or a sedative. Conversely, real healing intends to promote restoration, better results, and a healthier destination. Making it better in the end.

So, healing that's merely the *opposite* of decomposing or unhinging isn't really healing at all. This is because real healing is an act of 'completion'. A conscious choice to become whole again. Perhaps different, but whole nonetheless. For the hurt or loss will never truly go away. The pain is always there to a degree. So if we 'heal' without learning to live more fully 'with the pain', it's only making the pain stop. Stop only for the moment. And we're still in solitary confinement.

We only walk out of 'Solitary' when we move toward *Seeking*. Seeking is not existing or survival. It's not controlling. It's not making pain or loss go away in the narrow sense of healing. Instead, it's about giving the trauma or the suffering some meaning. About making our loss, guilt, shame, or pain actually mean something to us. By releasing it from the cement that it's encased within at the moment. Healing through seeking is not a destination, either. It's a process. Sometimes a long one, by the way. And it's never an easy one.

But it's an important one nonetheless. A process of iteratively gained insight, reflection, rehabilitation, and change. Just as the 'geniuses' of years ago thought solitary confinement would be like. But what they got so terribly wrong was this: their fervent belief that we can do this change alone. In fact, we can't. Solitude is important. Sometimes it's crucial to our journey of seeking. But solitude is an interlude. Not a long-term prison sentence. Especially when we self-impose it or allow others to do so on our behalf.

We embark on 'seeking' when we give expression of our being to others. In many simple and profoundly complex ways. Through our conversations. Our stories. Our words. Our interactions. Our outwardly shed tears. Conversely, we don't pursue seeking when we internalize our feelings. Or when we avoid them. When we flee. When we deflect. When we blame. Or seek revenge on another person. Or by our physically harmful releases of our hurt. Hitting a table or a wall may feel like it's 'letting off steam'. But it's not helpful. And hitting another solves absolutely nothing. It's an act of brazen aggression that only makes matters worse. Any of these negative tactics of human 'expression' may seem to assuage the pain, but they don't. And they're never acts of seeking. Not in any form.

In fact, the only way to truly 'seek' lasting healing is to engage. To engage with ourselves and with others. We engage when we cry out. Even if it's in a loud outside voice. We engage when we simply cry. Or when we sob. Or when we give words to our pain. Because this engagement means that we're seeking to give this pain a story. Seeking to give it a narrative. Seeking to create memories. Seeking verbal descriptions, however feeble they may seem to us. But, even more so, deep engagement tries to make some sense out of catastrophe. To provide some helpful meaning where possible.

Trying to find meaning is the key. Meaning making happens when we refuse to stop at verbal 'accountings' or re-accountings of the what's, why's, and how's of what occurred or what's currently going on. Meaning making happens when we courageously move beyond our stories and our narratives. Even beyond our stated feelings. It happens when we put symbols to our pain. Using phrases such as "This feels like a heavy stone has been placed on my chest" ... Such as "This hurts like an arrow has just pierced my heart" ... Or such as "It's almost as if the sun has permanently retreated behind the clouds." These kinds of words attempt to draw analogies. To make comparisons. To look backwards or sideways for similarities. To connect the dots as feasible.

This sounds like such a small step, to be sure. But, in reality, it's really deep progress. For when we seek meaning in pain and loss, we're finally stepping back from the brink. We're trying to look at ourselves and at our pain more realistically and fully. In the process, we're moving from *'Subject to Object'*. We're trying to make sense of it all. Trying to interpret it. Trying to find some meaning within it. In this important vein, we're also moving from 'Solitary' to the general population. Not just leaving our single prison cell to join the others in the jail. No. We're walking out the prison door altogether. To be free at last. To make a fresh start. Not one of forgetting. But one of healing in the midst of it all. With the general population. That means all of us. Out there. In the world.

Wrestling with God

On any given day in my past work as a hospital chaplain, I've met the 'actors' in the drama of chronic illness, dying, medical emergencies, and traumatic injuries. I have stood bedside with families when aggressive life support measures were withdrawn in favor of comfort care at the end of patient's lives. I've listened to the life stories of patients and their families as they've verbally recounted poignant memories of their loved-one's careers, achievements, disappointments and regrets, losses, fears, and hopes. I've also sat with those who are grieving a life just-passed.

In many of these emotionally challenging encounters, the patient's family unit was well functioning and supportive. In a number of others, though, the family struggled with the patient or amongst themselves. In these instances, the family's many dysfunctions were not ameliorated by the demands of caring for a sick loved one. No. Quite the opposite, in fact.

These dysfunctions were most often exacerbated, becoming even more fractious as a patient's medical condition and probable outcome deteriorated. Coping mechanisms, however maladaptive, were further strained—literally untethered in the midst of this family crisis. Sadly, at the very time that family unity and alignment mattered most, intra-family wrestling tended to fracture things even further.

So when things begin to unravel, we do too at times. We wrestle. Even harder than normal. Sometimes within our families. But sometimes *also* with God. Patients and families battle with their preexisting notions of God, now strained to the breaking point over a terminal diagnosis, a downturn in one's condition, or simply the enormous weight of a chronic, painful illness with no reasonable expectation of ever healing. The wrestling takes place not in a ring or on a mat in a gym. But it's a contest of doubt, perceived power, and persistence, nonetheless.

Wrestling with God is a common theme in the Bible. Even the heralded patriarchs of the 1st Testament faced their own moments of doubt with God. At times, they took matters into their own hands or schemed their way out of predicaments. In this regard, Jacob may be the 1st Testament character *most* emblematic of wrestling. He seemed to turn this into a 'science'. He was particularly noteworthy for his reliance on his own wits, pride, planning, charisma, self-confidence, and considerable material resources. There was one example after another in Jacob's life. A habitual 'wrestler' to be sure.

Pick up a Bible and read about Jacob. You'll recall that he wrestled with his brother, Esau, for his birthright much earlier in their lives. Jacob and his mother, Rachel, subsequently partnered to wrestle with Jacob's father, Isaac, for Isaac's blessing. As an adult, Jacob later wrestled with Laban for his daughter in marriage. Jacob also schemed to secure Laban's flocks before fleeing to return to his homeland. On his way home, Jacob wrestled again—this time, in the most noteworthy way ever. As the story goes, he was going home to reconcile with his estranged brother, Esau. Understandably, he was quite worried about how he'd be received, given their history of animosity over Jacob's past scheming.

On the way there, Jacob sent messengers ahead to curry favor with Esau. For example, Jacob instructed his advance party to acknowledge that Jacob would be bearing oxen, donkeys, and other flocks as gifts. Jacob hoped that these gifts would please Esau, and would pave the way for Esau's forgiveness. Jacob subsequently prayed (or some would say 'negotiated') with God—acknowledging his trepidation in returning home into his angry brother's lands. He feared for his own life and for those of everyone in his party. He reminded God of God's previous promises. He recalled that God had pledged to make his descendants as numerous as sand particles in the sea—far too many to be counted. As such, he entreated God not to go back on God's own prior commitments. He wanted God to make things right for him.

Next, Jacob schemed to create a strategic advantage against his brother, Esau, who was approaching with his own band of four hundred men. Jacob decided to send waves of servants with the actual animals and other offerings to appease Esau and to 'soften' his brother's resolve. But Jacob *also* knew that these gifts would slow the advance of Esau, as Esau's own entourage became increasingly encumbered. Further, Jacob separated himself from his wives, children, and everything else that he had in hopes that all might not be lost in any possible conflict with Esau. Jacob wanted his own plans and schemes to make things right for himself.

The night before the reunion with Esau, Jacob was a total wreck. Think for just a moment what he must have been feeling as he laid his head down to sleep that evening. He would have been terrified. He was exhausted. He was deeply worried about his family and himself. According to the story, Jacob fell into a dream about wrestling with God, who was portrayed as a 'man'. Jacob couldn't see the man, making his fear even greater in this fitful semi-sleep. But Jacob was also persistent. For the 'man' did not prevail against him. The 'man' called out to Jacob, "Let me go, for the day is breaking." But Jacob continued to hang on. He said, "I will not let you go unless you bless me." This was after the 'man' struck Jacob squarely on his hipbone. Jacob was undoubtedly washed out, but he still held on. His whole being was brought into an epic struggle with God. It was not merely a dream. He had been awake in some ways, wrestling with God.

But here's the key in this story: God *also* wrestled with Jacob. God hung on too. Jacob wrestled in order that God would bless him for his upcoming encounter with Esau. In the process, God did bless Jacob. At the same time though, God did not disclose God's name in response to Jacob's demands. But God did 'rename' Jacob. The Bible states, "Then the man said, 'You shall no longer be called Jacob, but Israel, for you have striven with God and with humans, and have prevailed.'" This was God's doing, not Jacob's. So, in the end, Jacob had struggled and striven with God. However, he couldn't do so unless God first let him. He couldn't do so if God had refused to let him engage in the first place. As such, God also wrestled with Jacob.

God's wrestling signified God's commitment to stay with Jacob (and with us) in the struggle and in the relationship. God bound himself to Jacob (and to us) at the point of Jacob's (and our) greatest vulnerability. In the process of approaching and wrestling with Jacob, God, in turn, drove Jacob to make his reckoning with God. Jacob could no longer evade the false 'truth' that he believed about himself: that he could survive or heal entirely by his own wits, deceptions, schemes, and cunning. Although now a bit lame, having been hit in his hip, Jacob was actually a far stronger person as a result of the encounter. Because Jacob could live with *less* dependence on himself, his own fitness, and his perceived capacity.

And what about us? As spiritual people, we also wrestle. We wrestle with the Transcendent One for help with our health, wellbeing, jobs, family members, and friends. At times, we wrestle for less serious things, like good weather for an upcoming outing, barbeque, or vacation. Or a favorable outcome in a football game over the weekend ahead. About almost everything, to be honest. And we wrestle with each other. We compete for grades in school, promotions at work, and positions in line at the grocery store. The fast lane on the highway in order to pass slower drivers. Even with yellow traffic lights in an effort to speed through intersections at rush hour, if we're honest.

So we wrestle. In so many, many ways every day. With ourselves. With our circumstances. With others. And with God. But not so much as God wrestles with us. God graciously approaches us and allows us to engage God in our struggles in order that God might work through them. To somehow transform the darkness, doubts, and fears that confront us in our human condition. And how do we respond? We're encouraged to remain open to God's presence in times of darkness, fears, losses, and struggles.

Our remaining open to God may entail some waiting. And sometimes God appears to be silent or absent. But, in fact, God hasn't abandoned us. Quite the contrary. God is wrestling with us. The reality is this: we're holding firmly onto each other. And while we may not receive the entire blessing that we've asked for, we will have seen God's face and prevailed. In so doing, God has given us a new name. A new or renewed meaning, purpose, strength, and healing for navigating our way forward in the darkness.

So, who or what are you wrestling with today? And who is wrestling with you?

Our Quest for Healing
What Kind of God are You, Anyway?

What if God is a God of Life? A real, breathing, living, and loving 'life'. Many of us don't know this God, I'm afraid. For, far too often, our religious faiths and stories are grounded in our sinfulness. With inherent flaws born into us. You know, from way back. From the beginning, actually. You remember Adam and Eve, don't you? The Garden of Eden debacle. In fact, we *do* remember. Painfully so. And we don't forget it, either. In fact, we live in existential fear, anxiety, and worry. About our own mortality. About the life-to-come. The here-after. Eternity. After we die. Someday in the future. So, we live to die. In an individual kind of way.

We talk about God's freely given grace, but we live as if we have to earn it back. With regularity and repetition. Each of us individually. So we track our indiscretions. We fret our doubts, our promises, and our errors. We work to act right, to live right, to be right, and to stay right. We live each moment to *'return'* into God's grace... to be 'healed' in God's critical eyes. As a result, some of us rationalize our suffering. We wear it as a badge of honor. The more the merrier. Bring it on. Because we must deserve our suffering in some perverse sort of way. Alternatively, we become angry when we feel that we can't measure up. Or when we stumble or fail along the way. Or we become judgmental of others in an effort to appear somehow better in our eyes. Or God's.

Here's the problem with all of this. As a result of our own self-absorbed and self-obsessed anxiety, too many of us utterly fail to see and heal the real, collective 'hell' within our very midst. The one we've created or adopted around our fear of God's disapproval of us. And our being shipped right off to Hell if we don't shape up. Pronto. In the process, we miss the needs around us right here. Right now. In *this* world, not the next one.

We do this because we misinterpret the nature of human 'salvation'. At least to an extent. We misrepresent salvation when we privatize it. When we make it about us, not about all of us collectively. We misuse the term when we view it as positioning us somehow for someday soon. Down the road. A single seat on a private life raft to Heaven. First class, in fact. For I'm 'saved' for tomorrow. We also malign salvation when we believe that it's an earned thing. Something that you can achieve. Even at the expense of someone else you've 'edged out' in some zero-sum contest. You know, the poor guy who'll be 'left behind'.

But we should take a minute and think about this. And ask ourselves some important questions about our underlying assumptions. Do we actually believe that an eternally loving, universally life-giving God is really concerned with this kind of background 'noise'? With things like taking tickets to the Pearly Gates some day in the future. With things like exactly who gets in and who is pushed out of the heavenly winner's circle. You know, in the future. What kind of God would actually worry about this stuff anyway? As such, ponder, for a moment, the kind of God that you worship and follow. Reflect on the intrinsic 'character' of the Divine.

Why would God create us only to destroy the vast majority of us at the end of time? Why would God create the world, only to neglect it in favor of some perfect future state? What kind of God deprioritizes human death, poverty, marginalization, destruction, starvation, disease and sickness, grief, and sorrow around us right now? And instead spends God's time keeping tallies of all our individual discretions? What kind of God supposedly loves us unconditionally while simultaneously dishing out human suffering as some payback or penance for falling off the individual salvation wagon? What kind of God would do this kind of stuff for goodness sake? If so, what kind of God are you, anyway?

So here's another 'take' on this story. What if God has created us to send us *all* out into the world? Not just the 'saved' people. But everyone who's willing to join in. And not for someday. But for right now. Finally, not as part of some celestial voyage to some far-way place called Heaven, resting comfortably in the clouds and the stratosphere. But for here on this earth . . . the one that God created for us in the first place. Here and with a real purpose. To live and to love and to work together. In peace. In 'just' fellowship and communion. Where everyone is welcome. And where every element of our lives matters to God in real time. In all of life's current fullness.

God's life in us is a divine healing light, sometimes flickering, sometimes burning brightly. *Our* job is to keep this light burning. To make it burn more brightly. To share it with others in harmony, community, fullness, healing . . . and love. This light is our compass, our guide, our truest self, and the very meaning of our lives. I mean 'life'. A God-filled and truly saved life. A just and interdependent life. I mean real life. Salvation life. Lived joyfully in *this* moment. Together. Now, that's a good story. God's. Not ours.

Freedom Through Forgiveness

The winter months can be stark. Grey. Misty. Cold. Leafless trees stand like rigid sentries against the dim skies of January. The angle of the sun is low. A tree's branches form intricate tentacles in silhouette. As we gaze upon the trees, it's easy to feel cut off, imprisoned, shut in, and alone. We're driven inside. Sometimes within ourselves.

The journey of forgiveness is a lot like this. When we don't forgive others, we're also imprisoned. Separated from life and from the living. Unable to see beyond the tall, stone walls only feet in front of us. Unable to see beyond the barbed wire stretched directly above the walls. Intricately woven wire. Like the barren branches in winter's leafless trees. A stark, foreboding silhouette. Against the dim, cloudy winter sky. Without love.

Now we say it all the time. "I forgive you." "You're forgiven." "I'm going to let it go." "Time will surely heal." "Let's forget about it and move on, shall we?" "I'm choosing to show leniency." "I'll let God judge his wrongs against me." We say these things. Over and over. And we honestly believe that we've forgiven the transgressor. Perhaps we've put the whole thing behind us. Perhaps we think that we've actually let it go. But it's still in front of us. It's still walking with us. It's still holding us. Or we're still holding onto it. And, as such, we're the victims two times. Once from the hurt inflicted on us. And a second time from the hurt that we continue to inflict on ourselves. All is not forgiven, after all.

We don't forgive until we affirmatively decide to do so. Then not until we do the actual work of forgiveness. This means that we acknowledge the hurt caused us by another. Yes, we have to 'own' and 'name' our feelings about the hurt . . . and the reasons for these feelings. Further, real forgiveness means that we try to enter into the 'life' and the heart of the one who's hurt us—attempting to see the hurt from the other's perspective. To walk in their shoes for a minute. To reflect on what might have been going on in the person who's transgressed against us. Perhaps their intent wasn't egregious at all. It's possible that they made an honest mistake.

Further, forgiveness means that we accept the hurt without the need for revenge or returning the hurt to another in some way. At some time. In some place. Of our choosing. Some day. In this sense, forgiveness means that it no longer matters whether the person deserves to be forgiven. Or not. Finally, doing the work of forgiveness means that we share our feelings with the other. Then communicate our forgiveness to him or her. Then extend compassion and good will to the other with proper, healthy 'boundaries' for us in the future. Even if we don't get an apology back. Ever.

The work of forgiveness is difficult. It's really, really hard. It can feel excruciating. It can take days or months or years or decades. Sometimes we can do it with our own resources. Sometimes we need help from others. Sometimes we choose not to forgive at all. Or to remain a victim. That's our choice. It may actually feel more comfortable doing things this way. Or seem to anyway. But, in the end, failing to forgive is a prison of *our* choice. A 'cancer' that grows within us. Until it consumes us. The person who hurt us may never care. But we should. About ourselves. For *we* have been hurt. And we need healing. From within.

Forgiveness is like a bird. Like a cardinal that 'lights' upon a naked, barren tree in the midst of a grey, misty winter day. Its brilliant color stands out ever-sharply against the colorless, dim background of the January skies. We notice the contrast of life as the cardinal's feathers paint a winged portrait of bright red. But something else happens here, too. The cardinal's presence changes everything around it. The colors of this avian 'visitor' seem to bring new light and life to all of the branches around the spot in which it has landed.

Our hearts lighten and soften as we see the bird. And then it flies away. When we choose to forgive others, we're like the cardinal on that cold, winter's day. We change everything around us for the better. Then we fly away. Not to flee, but to bring light and grace to someone else. In true freedom.

A Call to 'Arms' . . . and Legs

In his classic children's book, *The Happy Prince*, author Oscar Wilde recounts the meeting of a southerly migrating swallow and a statue of a happy prince at the outset of winter. The statue had once been a young boy, sequestered within a garden estate where everything that he saw was beautiful. Now, as a statue at the entrance to a city, he has experienced the misery of poverty and sickness all around him for the first time. And he is crying.

He befriends the swallow, convincing the bird, however reluctantly at first, to stay with him and remove the rubies, sapphires, and gold plating from his statue-body in order to provide them to the suffering people in the city. As winter sets in, his loyal friend, the swallow, dies from the cold (but in service to others) at the feet of the statue. Furthermore, the now-shabby statue is subsequently removed, disassembled, and melted. However, the statue's heart will not melt down and is discarded, along with the dead swallow, in the trash. God asks an angel to bring to God the most precious things in the city. The angel returns with the dead swallow and the happy prince's lead heart. God proclaims that, in God's garden of paradise, the bird will now sing for everyone. The happy prince will praise God's name forever.

The Happy Prince is not a typical Christian salvation story. Perhaps, however, it tells us something about sin and salvation. The story illuminates the violence of human rejection and resultant suffering. It portrays the loving and intricately woven bonds between friends. It speaks to us about our capacity to transform life, death, and rebirth right here in this world. For, like Wilde's happy prince, we stand, as humanity, before the 'city'. We are *all* made of gold, rubies, and sapphires. Not because we plated ourselves, but because God made us that way in God's own creation purpose. As we gaze across the city, we therefore see the joy inherent in the special sacredness of all humanity.

Yet we also see the pain and suffering in God's people. We see that some are wealthy, while others want for simple basics in their lives. We see that some are powerful, while others are oppressed. We see that some make themselves beautiful at the expense of others: the poor, the marginalized 'non-persons', the sick, and the lonely rejected 'souls' of the city. Unless we carefully listen, though, the cries of those left behind can hardly be heard. For in the face of this quiet suffering, the loud voices of ignorance, complicity, and compromise are almost deafening to the ear. Amidst this picture, the happy prince is crying. Many of us are crying too.

However, there is great hope amongst the tears. For, like the happy prince, we have been gifted with a heart– a heart from God with the capacity to love, forgive, heal, share, and help empower others. And fortunately, our hearts *can* melt. We can see our city with new, understanding, loving, and compassionate eyes: the very eyes that God gave us in creation. And, with this vision, our hearts will melt. As our hearts melt, they will be moved as well.

For, unlike the statue-prince, we are not lodged in stone. We can and must venture out in God's name. We can and must move into the city. We can and must stand in prophetic solidarity with those who suffer. We can and must selflessly share our own God-given gifts, sapphires, rubies, and gold. We can and must turn back to each other in true healing fellowship and community. It's all quite possible . . . if only we try together. And it's a redemptive, healing salvation we can all live with.

Closure: Trusting the Source

We've all looked into the clear blue sky on a sunny day and gazed at the long white lines that are periodically etched across it. If we look long enough, we'll see that the initial clarity and fineness of these lines begin to blur and widen. The sharpness and form begin to dissipate. Eventually, the lines disappear altogether if we watch with persistent patience. What we're seeing are 'contrails'. Contrails are clouds that are formed from water vapor released from a high-flying airplane in the sky. The plane's exhaust condenses and freezes in the air. Thus, becoming artificial clouds of sorts.

These contrail 'clouds' disappear when the vapor subsequently evaporates. The speed at which this evaporation occurs depends on the conditions in the atmosphere at the time. So it varies a good deal. As we look at contrails, many of us have pondered where they come from. Why does this happen? Why don't the beautiful and mysterious lines stay around longer in the sky? Further, did any of this actually happen *at all* if we can't see it anymore?

Closure is a lot like this for most human beings. We like to have things explained to us. We like everything tied up with a bow. Questions answered. Case closed. That's why we call it closure anyway, isn't it? But how can we get closure if things are left yet unsaid, undone, or with an outcome that we find qualitatively unsatisfactory? With promises seemingly not kept. With our normally 'acceptable', reliable sources hard to find. With lots of unsettling open-endedness around our beliefs, our dreams, our loved ones, our friendships, and even life itself. Especially when these have been seemingly lost to us forever.

Absolutely no one escapes the necessity of struggling with closure (or apparent lack thereof). Not even the disciples of Jesus Christ in the 2nd Testament of the Bible. Not even them. Picture this for a moment: Christ had just been crucified on The Cross. The worst form of execution-style death possible in the ancient world. The disciples must have been utterly terrified. Perhaps they were going to be 'next' for crucifixion. Even worse, this was not supposed to have happened in the first place. For they had believed that Christ was the coming Messiah 'in the flesh'. That all would be well. That the Roman Empire would now be crushed. And their rightful King, Jesus, would rule in peace for all eternity.

But their promised King had just been mercilessly executed in shame. And Christ's disciples must have felt betrayed, forsaken, lost, and saddened beyond words. They were actually in *disbelief*. The Book of Luke in the Bible's 2nd Testament offers some important insight in this regard. Luke states that women were the first to go to the tomb of Jesus. And they found a large rock rolled away from the tomb's opening.

More importantly, the women also discovered that the tomb was now empty. And they witnessed the appearance of two 'men' who verbally confirmed to them that Christ was no longer there. That Christ was Risen. The two 'men' reminded the women of what Jesus had already told them about his crucifixion and his subsequent rising. Reminded them of what they had *already* learned and actually knew underneath their grief and doubts.

The women returned to the remaining eleven male disciples and told them about this miracle. But the disciples didn't believe the women. The 'guys' thought it was only idle talk. From unreliable sources, given their narrow, paternalistic way of thinking. Ironically enough, two of Christ's disciples were walking to Emmaus on the very same day. As they traveled, they were talking about all the things that had just happened. At this time, a 'man' appeared and walked with them on the road. This 'man' reminded them of what Jesus had *already* told them about his crucifixion and rising. Reminded them of what they had *already* learned and actually knew underneath their grief and doubts.

As they neared the town, the disciples asked the 'man' to stay with them overnight and rest. And when they began to eat their meal together, the 'man' broke and blessed the bread. Then he gave it to them. Then the Bible says that their 'eyes were opened' and they recognized Jesus. But, at that very moment, Jesus vanished from their sight. The two disciples quickly got up and returned to Jerusalem, amazed at what had just transpired. And they said to each other, "Were not our hearts burning within us while he was talking to us on the road, while he was opening the Scriptures to us?" They subconsciously knew that the 'man' was Jesus before they visually recognized him. But they didn't understand this until after the fact.

So, the disciples were struggling mightily with closure on the death of Jesus prior to actually seeing the risen Christ with their own eyes. At a root cause level, their trust issues drove this struggle. The disciples didn't know who or what to trust in, frankly. For one, they didn't trust the women's initial account of Jesus' open tomb. Because women were unfairly dismissed as unworthy and uninformed in this historical culture. What's more, the disciples didn't trust their hopes, either. They didn't seem to trust what Jesus had previously told them about his need to suffer and die. Nor about Christ's promise to always be with them.

In fact, they didn't trust much of anything in the throes of their grief. Instead, they stubbornly held onto the hope that things might return to the way things were before. Prior to Christ's crucifixion. Just like old times again. That the death of Jesus was nothing more than a bad dream. And that Jesus would return in the flesh. And resume where they left off. In other words, they stood firm in *their* preconceived human notions about what was right and just. They wanted a reinstatement of what had been. In the exact way that they had understood it would be. In order to get some real closure in this.

But in truth, we can't have closure without real, heart-felt trust. The disciples had to have known this if they were listening to Jesus at all during their time with him. They must have understood this at some, albeit buried, level in their hearts. We know it, as well, if we dig deep enough. In the end, trust is foundational to our spiritual being and to healing. So, given the foundational importance of trust, what is it actually? According to the 2nd Testament book of Hebrews, trust is what we call 'faith'. Per Hebrews, "Faith is confidence in what we hope for and assurance about what we do not see". Now this definition is all well and good as it goes. But, with all due respect, there are some problems with looking at trust in this way.

First of all, faith (or trust) seems to be primarily future focused in Hebrew's way of defining the term. It's future facing. Based on hope and expectancy. Second, it seems to imply assurance. As if our faith requires conviction, certainty, and being convinced of something. Third, it seems to imply something tangible. We have faith in something's existence in real form. Or an action that will be taken. Lastly, this kind of faith looks to something outside of us. External to us. Instead of within us. At a heart level.

That's not to say that we should never trust in something external. But sometimes we simply have to trust our *own* hearts. Not our guts. Not our senses. Not even our logic or our intellect. We need to lean into what's already within us. In other words, we have to Trust the Source. Like when we see a vivid contrail in the sky on a bright sunny day. We can't trust that it will hold its exact shape for long. Because it won't. We can't trust the atmosphere around the contrail, for it is inherently fickle. It will do with the contrail what it wishes in the end. And the contrail will, in fact, disappear in the end, as well. As such, the contrail isn't the source. The airplane is.

On a far more practical level in our own 'spiritual' healing, we can trust the only important source: God. To be sure, we trust not primarily in what God has done or continues to do. But in what God has *already* told us. Even more importantly, we trust in God's character of love. Because, in the end, this is the only real source of closure for us. When the 'atmosphere' around us churns up our lives, blurs the lines, and dissipates our clarity about things. Therefore, we have to get past our reliance on all things tangible, future, and action-oriented in order to heal with closure.

Next, we have to push our existing five senses as human 'beings' far more to get outside of our own boxes. To get out of our own way at times. Then develop a healing, spiritual 'sixth sense' in order to actively reach for the knowledge and learning already imparted to us by God. Just like Jesus tried to do with his disciples. This new, sixth sense is the ability to navigate within the often murky spaces of our lives. The capacity to trust in our own hearts. To trust in our respective places in the universe as given to us by God. To trust in our souls. Our internal compasses. Our conscious and unconscious enlightenment, knowledge, and spirituality.

Depending on how long and how deeply this sixth sense has been buried in our lives, we may have to dig for a while. Shovel it out. Uncover it. Surface it. Rediscover the source. But please know this: everything you need is there for the finding. And the reward is peace. Closure with healing peace. Real closure. Even when reality, as we knew it, appears to have disappeared. Like the contrail in the sky.

'Quest'-ions for Prayer and Further Reflection

- How are you 'wrestling' with God and with others in your sorrows, pain, and setbacks of daily life? How do your beliefs about God and God's inherent character help or hurt your healing process?
- What areas of your life need to be restored around greater internal peace, grace, love, and 'being'? Conversely, who needs *you* to help show them a more hopeful, trusting, grace-filled, and peaceful example in actualizing God in them, as well?

- In what ways do you engage or distance yourself from the suffering of others? What's really going on underneath your responses in this area?
- What gets in the way of your practicing greater grace and forgiveness in your life? How can you begin to address these hindrances in order to enjoy greater freedom for yourself and for others?
- Who and what do you most trust in your life? How healthy and spiritually helpful are these sources, if you're completely honest with yourself?

Our Quest for Transcendence

Transcendence:

- *Existing beyond expected, existing, or normal levels*
  - *Exceeding accepted limits*
- *Outstretching our current abilities to understand*
  - *Bigger than the sum of its parts*
    - *Achieving a superior state*

Manifest Destiny

WHILE IT WAS NEVER a rigid doctrine with a fully agreed-upon set of principles, the idea of *Manifest Destiny* had its genesis in the early 19th Century in the United States. It is based on the notion that the U.S. was an exceptional nation. That we possessed unique and admirable virtues as a people. That *our* vision of democracy and *our* institutions were truly remarkable ones. This idea implied our inherent greatness, both real and potential. Both present and future. And taken to its next logical extension, this greatness had to be shared and encouraged elsewhere within the world. Everywhere, in fact.

Our bounden duty was to show others *the* way. To fulfill the destiny of all people, wherever located globally, in *our* transcendent, exceptional image. Adopting our transcendent, lasting values. But while such values as individual freedom, free enterprise, democracy, and the American dream were (and are) certainly admirable, the notion of Manifest Destiny has been far too often used as a heavy stick in our history. In other words, we've failed to stop at sharing and talking about them with others. Instead, we've imposed them on others when they 'failed' to see things our way.

For example, the confiscation of Native American lands and the forced confinement of these people on reservations were, all too often, rationalized away as part of the unbounded westward expansion of our nation during the 19th century. Further, we rallied around the purchase of territories and a war with Mexico in order to annex the Southwest. Then we overran and settled this land in the name of our exceptional way of life. In many ways, then, our country's current geographic boundaries are based largely on the historical application of Manifest Destiny.

To be fair, the U.S. celebrates numerous endearing qualities. It's a place of opportunity, liberty, and freedom for many people. We're governed by a long-standing Constitution, by the rule of law, and by the orderly, peaceful transfer of power. Further, there are any number of exceptional aspects around our way of life, our communities, and the notion that anyone (at least in theory) can succeed. And we're right to share this story within and outside the United States. There's much to celebrate and to appreciate. Where we run afoul, however, is when we *impose* this vision on others. When we strive to build other nations in our own image, however messy or unsettling the process.

It's even more dangerous, however, when we use *God* as the basis for it. When we do violence to others, either internally or externally, in God's name. Or in the name of any religion or sectarian religious beliefs. Doing so is wholly un-spiritual. It degrades us as human beings. It also disgraces God in the process. Nonetheless, we sometimes do it with destructive and disastrous results. But why? Well, in many respects, the problem lies in our beliefs about God. Because I'm writing primarily from a Christian context, I'll use the Bible as a specific example to illustrate this.

Without a doubt, the Bible is a marvelous, timeless book—full of theology, guidance for living, and stories. Sadly, though, some of our Biblical stories are *also* rife with violence by some against others. Of battles and conflict. Of physical, bloody conquests. Of abusive sexual violence against women and children. Of the brutal enslavement of some by others. And we've sometimes used the Bible in ways that try to justify this kind of violence. That attempt to justify the bondage of slaves. That have rationalized away the marginalization of those of lesser status or power.

But what makes this Biblical interpretative process *most* harmful is our tendency to actually attribute much of the heavy-handedness in the

Bible's stories to God. For if we believe that the Bible is God's unalterable, undeniable, unquestionable, and perfect words, then God must be responsible for at least some of this violence. For God is seen as partnering in it, at times. Now to be fully fair, God also gave voice to the 1st Testament prophets. Voices of justice, of compassion, and of truth. And God *did* punish people for their hypocrisy, their untruths, and their sinful actions. But God's acts of anger and punishment can also, in turn, appear to make God a violent and harsh judge.

In the end, the utter messiness of it all lies in *our literal* interpretation of the Bible. Reading it as if it's all on God's back. It's all in God's hands. Using God's own literal words. Then using these words to perpetrate God's supposed vision onto others. In so doing, though, *we're* the problem. Not God. For when we impose our way of thinking and living onto others, we try to neatly explain away our own oppressive behavior by using the Bible as our shield. And that's a 'non-starter' in my book. We cannot rationalize un-spiritual, unloving, and subsuming behavior based on words and acts that we somehow believe God would condone. On the basis of Manifest Destiny as entitled peoples, religious groups, or via various exclusive, 'sacred' principles.

So why do we sometimes do this? The famous psychiatrist Sigmund Freud developed the principle of *'Transference'* many years ago. He argued that we 'transfer' or redirect our feelings and desires toward someone or something else on occasion. Most often, these feelings are unconscious and not-yet surfaced, but are present nonetheless. They may have germinated from much earlier in our lives, including our difficult experiences from our childhoods or our families of origin. Transference is triggered when someone or something reminds us of these unconscious or repressed experiences and feelings.

For example, someone may do something that subconsciously reminds us of an incident much earlier in our lives. About something done to us by an entirely different person long ago. At times, it's a reminder of something good or pleasant. Very often, though, it reminds us of something hurtful or anxiety-producing *in our past*. When this happens, we might project unwarranted and unconscious anger, resentment, or fear onto the person we're engaging with *now*. Onto a person who has absolutely nothing to do with our repressed memory issues from our past. Not the one who's actually responsible for our underlying feelings in the first place.

Alternatively, we might experience something now that causes us to *repeat* a behavior that we've used with some regularity in the past to cope with our unconscious and buried memories. For instance, we might respond to a current situation by fleeing or beginning to cry. Or by feeling fearful. Or by experiencing a tightening in our throat. And we do so for no apparent reason. Our behaviors now are merely a regurgitation of some maladaptive coping mechanism from our past. We can't explain why we're reacting in this unhealthy way, but we are nonetheless. It's a misdirected 'repeat performance' out of unconscious habit.

So, marrying Freud's principles with Manifest Destiny, what if our need to control things, people, places, or things is a tangible example of transference on our respective parts? And taken to the next level, what if our need to use God as an excuse for this actually constitutes transference of our own anxieties onto God, as well? We conquer, impose, and sometimes even hurt others—then attribute it to God or God's Word. We project our own insecurities or our distorted moral sense of our exceptionality (at another's expense) onto God. Then we make God responsible somehow. To the extent that we do so, its genesis lies within ourselves, not with God.

When we project onto others (or even God) in this way, it could be symptomatic of a critical root cause: non-differentiation. Murray Bowen developed important, seminal thinking around family systems theory. Bowen, and others who followed, have argued that *'Differentiation of Self'* is crucial to our human development and wellbeing. When we're appropriately differentiated, we're able to see ourselves as independent, self-sustaining, and well-centered persons. We live with others in healthy, mutually supportive ways.

But we're not dependent on other people or on circumstances external to us for our care, our sustenance, or our self-identity. In other words, we don't need others to 'complete us'. Nor do we need to impose ourselves on others. Conversely, though, when we lack differentiation (whatever the cause) or are unwilling or unable to develop it, we often act in ways that attempt to control others or to over-function on their behalf. Or we try to 'fuse' our own identities and needs onto others. We lose proper boundaries with other people and with other things.

What's the import of all this? What's the main point here? In the end, our need to impose on others, however we try to justify it, has much to do with the work we need to *first* do on ourselves. Behaviorally, for sure. And perhaps spiritually, as well. As spiritual people, we are 'of' God. But

God creates each of us as unique and special persons. We're beautifully and wonderfully made, in fact. Not to be fused with God, because we can't be. Not to be fused with others, because we shouldn't be.

As such, when we act in ways that transfer our own anxieties, insecurities, and past unconscious histories onto others (or even onto God) in the 'spirit' of Manifest Destiny, it rarely ends well. When we fail to take ownership as fully differentiated human beings, it doesn't end well, either. And when we generalize these behaviors into larger groups or entire societies, it ends very badly every time. Especially when we try to base it on God or God's word.

So, what if we looked to God with wider eyes? What if we looked more inclusively for the spark of God in others? Instead of simply what we *think* we're supposed to believe about them. What if we respected the uniqueness of others? If we respected the place, space, and full personhood of others? And put the notion of Manifest Destiny away. Deeply in a drawer somewhere. For Manifest Destiny was a questionable idea to start with, if we're honest. It was (and still is) interpreted very badly in real, actual human behaviors that hurt countless others.

Most importantly, though, it simply makes no sense. For *each of us* has a manifest destiny: the potential to live life fully and completely in dignified, differentiated, and conscious ways. In ways that facilitate our own discoveries along the way. *Manifestly our way.* Our own *Destinies.* Not the ones imposed on us by God or each other.

Immersion Conversion

Individual conversion is an integral part of Christian tradition and practice. It often refers to our turning away from sin. And our turning toward God. Some argue that this 'turning' requires our repudiation of not just our sins, but of our sinful self, as well. Down to the core. Repentance is a requisite. As is a 'cleansing'. Some traditions do this cleansing as part of infant baptism. Others baptize only older individuals, who must first profess a desire for forgiveness and belief in Jesus Christ.

With respect to baptism, some believe we can assertively desire and decide on it, based on having heard the Gospel and our expressing our faith in Christ. Others argue that the very act of 'saving' is based solely on God's determination. We're predestined for God's Kingdom or we're not. As such, our being saved is the manifestation of God's already-made, preordained choice. In either event, the actual sacrament of baptism varies in how it's carried out. Some religious traditions do it via sprinkled water. Others fully immerse the new believer in water, often in a baptismal pond or even a lake. Upon surfacing, the believer is cleansed, saved, and redeemed.

I acknowledge that the cynic in me may be coming out here. While I find deep meaning in infant baptism as a sacramental *reminder* of God's love, a celebration of new life, and the welcoming of a new member to any church community, I'm left wondering about the mystical efficacy of 'saving' anyone who has absolutely no idea of what's actually going on—especially with respect to an innocent baby. I'm thinking that the baby already has it all over the rest of us jaded souls. As for adolescents and adults, I value thoughtful decisions to turn toward a more God-filled life.

Sadly, though, I've witnessed and heard about far too many deathbed and crisis-led confessions and conversions that lead to 'in the moment of trial' baptisms. And I struggle to characterize these baptisms as truly 'saving' anyone in that moment. All too often, priests and other clericals are called in for last-minute rituals and sacraments. Now, acts of cleansing, forgiveness, and absolution by clergy can certainly ease the 'sinner's' sense of fear and loathing in his or her final breaths. They can provide a sense of unquestioned comfort in the face of a crisis. In its worst forms, however, they're little more than a feel-good exercise for everyone involved by an ordained 'someone' purported to have sacramental, surefire forgiveness-bearing privileges. Affording superficially perceived relief that a one-way ticket to Heaven has actually been issued. And just in time without a second to lose. Whew! Our bases are now covered.

However well intended, the whole notion of religious conversion, more broadly, is often misconstrued and misused. We throw the term around at our peril when we fuse other things into or onto it. Conversion is harmful when it leaves others out. You know, the 'unsaved'. I've often found this uncomfortable when, as a Chaplain in the past, I was periodically asked whether 'I was saved'? I'm uneasy with the question precisely because I'm not sure what to do with it, if I'm honest. Saved from what? Saved to what? About which aspects or elements of me? The implication is that I'm either saved or I'm rotting. Like vegetables or uncooked meat in the refrigerator. If I say that I'm saved, I'm not sure what it implies. How am I supposed to act differently if I am?

I already try to live my life in accord with God's principles and light. And I'm changing and growing in my faith. Most importantly, however, I believe that God created me *already* 'saved'. I simply need to live my life making the very most of this God-given grace and love each day. Why isn't that good enough, anyway? For comparison purposes, I do look around and see lots of people who argue that they're 'saved'. But they seem to have the same issues, problems, losses, behavioral challenges, family relationship issues, and shortcomings that I do. We're all working on them as best we can. They don't escape troubles and suffering any more than I do. We all experience trials, no matter how 'saved' we may feel we are at any given moment.

And frankly, the whole notion of renouncing my inherent, willful, already baked-in sinfulness is troubling to me. It's like I have to give up on 'me' in order to become me. Like needing to send myself through a meat grinder in order to make some fancier kind of sausage. But if I do so, what's left of me? What's left of what God made in me with love in the first place? So, in a sense, conversion implies that I need to reject myself in some manner before I'm 'cleansed'. Conversion is at its worst, though, when we use this process to force change on other people. Along agreed, entrenched practices and rituals. In order to 'get them right with the Lord' too. The message here is clear: get on board or get off our train.

Given the aforementioned negatives, what if there's another way to think about 'conversion'? This other way would involve a continuous process. An ongoing, honest, and personal self-assessment of 'who' we are. And where we are. And how we need to incrementally keep growing in our spirituality and our 'being'. Rather than an epiphany event or a rousing chorus of "I've seen the light. Hallelujah", it might rest, instead, in some reflection and queries. Introspective questions such as what do I actually believe and why? What do I value in my life and why? What kind of person do I want to become and to be in the future? What changes might be helpful in tracking more fully toward this vision of God-filled love?

In this way, conversion can become a disciplined, daily practice of continuous change, growth, and inward transformation. A journey that keeps on going without a hard stop at some established denominational milepost. In this regard, we might find ourselves looking outwardly toward other persons, things, problems, and opportunities with truly different eyes for the first time. With a changing perspective. Not simply change for change sake. Not simply superficial change.

No. That which we're moving toward must be something *far more* substantial. Bigger than us, individually speaking. It has to be something that makes a real, positive, and lasting difference in us and in others around us. As such, conversion is less about believing in something or someone for the first time. Less about eureka moments. Less about ditching our old friends for new, 'saved' ones. Less about our personally adopting something like a creed, belief, or dogma as part of our 'toolbox of being'. Even less about answering in the affirmative to a scripted set of questions asked by someone else in some sacramental ceremony.

Real conversion is an all-encompassing, immersive experience. It consists of clearly and consistently embracing a set of important values or principles. Targeted toward fully integrated ways of 'being'. Some religious traditions have done a notable job in that respect. The Quaker Friends expend a significant focus on values such as simplicity, stewardship of our planet, integrity, equality, community, and peace. Following the Quaker Way is, therefore, far less about dogma. And far more about the kind of people we're becoming as a result of our faith. Far less about dictates and sacraments. And far more about queries, reflection, and challenge.

Phillip Gulley's book, *If The Church Were Christian*, is also helpful in this regard. He argues that the church's integrity with respect to their messages-versus-actions is sometimes inadequate. He calls for Christian churches to more fully live as Christ lived, not simply through our worship of Jesus. Gulley calls us to focus more on our potential as believers than on our existence as sinners. To practice more forgiveness and grace. In turn, to practice less judgment and less condemnation of others. To focus more on action and less on dogma. To hold a greater spirit of inquiry versus trying to hold the 'answers'. To foster more diverse thinking . . . and less conformity. Finally, to emphasize what happens outside the church's walls far more than maintaining the church institution itself.

If the church and its members would do so, we'd see not simply a return to the values of Jesus. But rather a real, substantive *Immersion Conversion*. In a world of Immersion Conversion, we'd minimize the rigid, 'righteous' credos that we all too often live in contradiction to. We'd see far less 'proof-texting' of the Bible in order to justify subtle (or open) discrimination against and submission of marginalized persons. Proof-texting happens when we handpick a Biblical passage in order to prove our pre-existent assumptions. In the process, we typically take the passage out of context or without using it properly within the broader theme or message of the overarching story.

In a world of Immersion Conversion, we'd see far less hypocrisy around key issues, such as Right to Life. Like when we purport to hold *all* life sacred—then focus entirely on anti-abortion causes. And, in turn, put the health and life of expectant mothers at risk when we force them to use unsafe, back-alley abortion providers. Or when we somehow try to justify capital punishment in murder cases, while conveniently forgetting that the state is killing the inmate here. Or when we forget about the actual quality of life for the poor all around us. Or tolerate human violence by extremists because they happen to support our specific religious-political agendas. What in the world is Right to Life when all lives don't matter?

In a world of Immersion Conversion, we'd also stop trying to demonize persons with different sexual orientations. Quit trying to subtly or otherwise exclude them from our congregations and our sacraments. As if they're freaks of nature somehow, not really 'normal' people with a right to participate and engage. In a world of Immersion Conversion, we'd stop defending our right to have and to use guns as some sacred, God-given privilege . . . at a time when our out-of-control gun culture has created bloody 'killing fields' on our very streets. With Immersion Conversion, we'd stop the hypocrisy of going to church on Sunday to worship life as God intended—then live Monday-Saturday as if it didn't really matter at all.

There *is* a better, more holistically immersive way. And here it is: to experience a real, lasting Immersion Conversion experience as spiritual, transcendence-seeking people. Converted to real, transcendent values. Not just beliefs and dogma. If we were more fully 'converted' in this sense, we'd be more passionate about our spirituality, not just our religion. We'd feel more joined-up and integrated as people, as well. Additionally, we'd fight and bicker far less with other religious sects and amongst ourselves. We'd experience our lives less anxiously. We'd look over our shoulder less often. Less worried about whether we're doing the details properly according to 'code'.

We might even be more peace-filled. More loving toward others. Less judgmental. And more open to people who look different. Who believe differently about the specifics of faith. You know . . . be willing to look beneath the surface level for a change. Because we *all* share some common core values and principles. Like the one about love, for example. We'd become better at more deeply and analytically examining our own respective faith traditions. Become less rigid and possessive while also becoming more open to new ideas. Less 'binary' (Yes/No; Right/Wrong; Good/Bad) and more multi-dimensional. In other words, we'd be more interested in questions and in pondering the mystery of things.

Finally, Christians would no longer stop at asking, "What would Jesus do?" They'd also ask the critical follow-on question: "*Why* would he do it in this way?" As a result, we'd live far more within the spirit of the law, not simply based on the letter of the law. In so doing, we'd change and stretch and grow more fluidly. We'd memorize less and analyze more. We'd embrace the many nuances and intersections of the world's many faiths, not just our own at the moment.

To be clear, we can be *both* religious and values-based spiritual people at the same time. The two aren't mutually exclusive. But for religion to be truly meaningful, well integrated, and world changing, our religious creeds must be grounded firmly in well-articulated human values, universal love, and respect for others. Then applied consistently and compassionately. If not, our religions are nothing more than clubs with special 'passwords', member-only handshakes, different club initiation rituals, and the favorite goodies shared by members after worship services. We deserve so much more than that. We need so much more than that. And God wants so much more than that. For us. So how about an Immersion Conversion?

Salvation Story at the 'Cross'-Roads

As people of faith, we're asked to be sacramental persons of waiting, honest introspection and reflection, sacrifice, and love. In the Christian tradition, The Cross of Christ is prominent. We're reminded of Jesus' sacrifice and his crucifixion on our behalf. Reminded about the wait between Good Friday and Easter Sunday. We often think about *these* specific aspects of Christ too much, though. Unfortunately, we do so at the cost of losing the historical Jesus—Jesus as a practicing Jew. The person of Jesus who came to be with us. To actually live with us. Who looked to 1st Testament Scripture for his teaching and his guidance to his followers. Who spoke with prophetic truth-to-power. Who walked the dusty paths in an unorthodox ministry outside the walls of mainstream cultural and religious acceptance.

With specific respect to Christ's death on The Cross, Christians have been taught any number of theories about its import to us. One view is that The Cross was (and is) substitutionary, with Christ having taken on our failings and our faults. As if Jesus stepped in for us. Took the fall in our place. Took on all our sinfulness and laid it on The Cross for us. Alternatively,

Our Quest for Transcendence

other theologians have taught that the Crucifixion was an epic battle between Christ and the Devil. Where Christ won. Where the power of evil was sentenced to death at the end of time. Evil is still here, but we're freed from Satan's power by our faith in the meantime.

But what if we looked at The Cross in yet a different way still? That *we* killed Christ. We all did. And we still do every day. Even now. All these years later. For we figuratively 'kill' Christ when we betray our Christian faith. When we reject the real message of Christ in our lives. When we turn our backs on Christ's historical, challenging 'living' messages of love and mercy and hope. When we forsake the Jewish principles of the Jubilee Year—a celebration of Sabbath rest, yes. But, more importantly, a call to renew our commitments around equality, social justice, and the forgiveness of debts. And the emancipation of all those held in slavery or in prison. The resumption of ownership to one's own familial lands via the return of property to its original owners.

A number of scholars argue that these concrete manifestations of the Jubilee weren't some casual, ancillary, or 'cameo appearance' type of reminders from Jesus. Instead, they were at the *very core* of Jesus' thinking and ministry. The idea of the Jubilee Year was the way of 'Shalom'—a Hebrew word with deep and significant meaning around human existence in states of peace, harmony, wholeness, wellbeing, and connectedness. They mattered back then. They still do today. And when we ignore these Jubilee principles, we simultaneously ignore the import of Christ's actual life. A 'saving' life that matters profoundly for us all . . . and for all times.

That said, if Christ's life 'saves' us more than his crucifixion could ever do, what difference does his death make? I argue that the death of Jesus accrues its greatest meaning in its revelatory nature. For The Cross served to embody the ultimate potential of human rejection, hate, fear, violence, and death in the name of God. Acts of demonizing, hurting, and killing others in God's name for God's sake. What in the world are we thinking, anyway? This is simply crazy. What's more and worse, these behaviors have continued unabated throughout subsequent human history. They pile one-on-another in our unfolding disgrace as people of many faiths around the world.

But The Cross *also* personifies something far more positive and hopeful. For it demonstrates God's enduring love for us in the face of our human rejection of God. God didn't walk away from us in the face of our most grievous, murderous crime against God's own Son on The Cross. Instead,

God responded through resurrection. This resurrection turned hate into love, renewal, and promise. Resurrection transformed death into life. Christ's resurrection validated and transformed the very meaning and life of Christ to a disbelieving world. The Risen Christ demonstrated once and for all that God's love was (and is) stronger than our hate. More powerful than our fears. Absolutely *nothing* was (and is) outside God's love. And this literally transformed the world—past, present, and future.

So what does this mean in terms of our salvation? If Christ's death (and God's steadfast love) were revelatory in the primary sense, how does The Cross translate into spiritual life for us? It does so in any number of ways, in fact. If we figuratively 'die to ourselves' for others in love, Christ's death brings life. If our own actions doom rejection, oppression, and separation in the world, Christ's death brings life. If our own work helps to actualize the liberating death of despair and the birth of renewed hopefulness for all, Christ's death brings life. If we end our own violence and the devaluation of all life, Christ's death brings life.

And what's more, it brings true life . . . thanks to the wonders of God's enduring love and grace. Where human hopes intermingle and intermix in joyful songs of peace and salvation. I can live with that!

Engaging a Faint Voice

To the victors go the spoils. Throughout our long human history of conflict, the winners get the spoils. Far too often, the victors of invasions, conquests, and battles subsequently and brutally subjugated their vanquished victims. With executions, pillaging, rapes, and kidnappings. Conquered villages were sometimes burned or otherwise destroyed. Prisoners were rounded up or simply shot on the spot. Women were taken as slaves or concubines. Children were absconded with or were simply abandoned to an orphaned life or slow starvation and neglect. These kinds of spoils in history are real, visual, and visceral. They should leave us shaken and aghast as we read about them. About how the winners have overwhelmed and eliminated those whom they've vanquished. And still do today.

A far more subtle, but equally pernicious, form of 'spoils-taking' goes on as well, though. While it's less noticed, it exerts a powerful and marginalizing influence on its victims. For this iteration of 'vanquishing the vanquished' informs our very sense of history itself. Our very understanding of what actually happened in the past. Because history is written by the victors. Those who win on history's stage write the books to a large extent. They get to tell the story. And although the story may be generally factual and even somewhat accurate overall, the nuances and details are dramatically influenced by the 'spin' created by the writers.

Even more importantly, the writers decide which portions of the story are actually told. Conversely, though, they *also* decide what components are left out. When they leave out important details or 'shade' these details to portray their cause in a better light, these writers steer readers of history in powerful ways. As such, what we've come to believe as being true may not actually constitute truth at all. In some ways, then, our history can become what we currently call 'fake news'. Made up. Papered over. Details omitted. Glorified accounting. Embellished. To make the victors look better, no matter how messy the actual reality was years ago.

An even more subtle form of 'spoils-taking' entails minimizing certain voices in what's written. Now let's be honest. The voices of the 'less powerful' in conflicts rarely make it to the front page of our history books. In fact, they're often marginalized, even if their own accounting of events is included at all as truthful in any sense. This is the case in history books. Within the countless volumes of theology on the stacks at most Christian seminary libraries. From the pulpits of too many churches and cathedrals on Sunday mornings. And it's no less true in the timeless, revered book of the Bible. Even the Bible, I'm afraid.

At the risk of offending those who honestly believe that this foundational book was literally dictated by God, most Biblical scholarship credits the Bible's books to human authors. These authors were divinely inspired in many important ways, no doubt. But they wrote their Biblical passages with specific audiences and goals in mind. They wrote from their particular experiences, histories, and contexts. They composed from verbal stories passed along generationally, in some cases for centuries on end. Further, the books of the Bible didn't magically 'land' in the Good Book. Human beings in history made crucial choices about what was 'in' and what was 'out' of Holy Scripture.

What's more, a relatively few persons actually made these calls. Not really a democracy. In fact, those who did so were all male. For males held a significant measure of theological or religious power. They were the clear victors in a class-based, patriarchal society. In contrast, those on the outside (including women, children, servants, and the poor) were the passive recipients of 'what the guys decided' in this regard. For that matter, even males who argued strenuously for opposing viewpoints and theologies were generally dismissed as somehow 'way out there'. Out of line. Sometimes, they were also excommunicated or were exiled. Or tortured. Or executed. To the victors go the spoils.

So what does this mean when we pick up a book like the Bible? It signifies that we're reading passages selected *for* us. By other people long ago. By persons with a certain perspective and context. And written with a lens of the historical, values-based, and social norms and rules at that time. As such, we'd be prudent to read the Bible with our own lens, as well. And with the knowledge that some 'voices' in the passages were maximized or minimized in a purposeful way. Maximized or minimized to reflect the historical author's beliefs or to tow-the-line of the victors. Or as subsequently edited in order to further the victor's agenda.

There's no better Biblical account to illustrate this predicament than the story of Mary and Joseph, the parents of Jesus in the 2nd Testament. Joseph was a male in a culture that amplified the role and power of fathers. But we honestly know little about him. In Hollywood terms, he got a 'bit part' in the story. An 'extra', of sorts, within the larger cast. In a cameo role. As such, it's easy to read right past him in the sweeping, evolving narrative around Jesus. But what if we were to re-read the story of Christ's birth from Joseph's perspective? To wonder and ponder how *he* must have felt. To listen to his faint voice.

We can only guess, but it might go something like this as Joseph anxiously considered Mary's unplanned pregnancy . . . especially inasmuch as they had not yet had sex. Joseph might have said, "How could this have happened? I've tried to live an upright life. I've done nothing wrong here. But Mary is now pregnant. Has she been unfaithful to me? She tells me that an angel appeared to her and placed a child, the Messiah, in her womb. But who will actually believe that story? Come on. I'm beside myself with doubt and questions. For, if I stay with Mary, we'll *both* be disgraced. But if I leave her, she'll be shunned as a sinful woman. Bad choices abound."

Joseph may have continued, "All I know is that the child is not mine. And frankly, I'm nearly paralyzed with fear. This is a complete mess. I've had a dream and have been told 'do not be afraid'. For our new son is to be called Jesus and he will 'save his people from their sins'. On the one hand, this comforts me. For it eases my conscience about staying with Mary. But, on the other hand, I'm still terrified. This isn't the way that new marriages are supposed to get off the ground." Now, of course, you'll find none of

Our Quest for Transcendence

this dialogue in the Bible. But it's interesting to wonder what Joseph was actually thinking. We'll never know, though, for his voice was faint in the written word. To the victors go the spoils.

And what about Mary's voice? How ironic that the person whom some call 'The Mother of God' had relatively few speaking lines in this unfolding Biblical drama. That a character venerated so highly in some religious traditions played a generally minor part in the written narrative. This isn't to say that Mary's role was, in fact, minor. Some go as far as claiming that she was born immaculately pure, without sin, in order to subsequently carry and give birth to Jesus Christ. Others carry this even further, insisting that she remained so. Ever-virgin in her marriage. Her husband, Joseph, wouldn't have been all that happy about this, I imagine. However, it's hard to even speculate about Mary's life as wife and mother. Because we read very little about her in the Bible.

But what if the 2nd Testament Biblical giant, Mary, had gotten a bigger speaking part in the Gospels? What might have been going on with her? As a parent. Like any mother of a newborn child. She might have said something like this. "You said what, God? I'm somehow pregnant with your Son? If so, then now what? How are Joseph and I supposed to properly raise your child? Joseph and I are simple people. We've never sought the spotlight here. We've never been seen as somehow 'different' amongst our family and community. Soon, everything will change."

Some years later, she might have gone on to say, "I feel completely incapable of dealing with all this coming change. Jesus is just a young boy, but he already knows more about sacred Scripture and law than I do or ever will. He understands more than practically everyone else, for that matter. I'm overwhelmed by the fact that my son is already way smarter than the adults around him. In fact, Joseph and I have to treat Jesus differently in *every* way. Both in terms of parenting him and in how he interacts with others. For example, God, how should Jesus' brothers and sisters in our family play with him? How should they jostle and wrestle with the Son of God?"

She might have concluded, "Most importantly, though, how will the world receive our son in the end? I'm humbled and am joyful, God, that you have chosen me as Christ's mother. But I worry about Jesus day and night. I pray that he will change the world for the better and will save our people. For he is the promised deliverer of peace. But he may not bring peace to *this* house in the process. Others may be afraid of him, his teachings, and his works. And reject him. And us. What is to become of all this,

God?" Of course, you'll find none of this in the Bible. But it's interesting to wonder what Mary was thinking. We'll never know, though, for her voice was faint in the written word. To the victors go the spoils.

Christians are right to focus first and foremost on Jesus Christ. But, in so doing, we should also remember the humanity of the other characters around Christ, as well. And when we pick up the Bible, it's helpful to read each story multiple times. No matter the story. To 'take on' the characters that aren't featured in the passages that we're reading. To put yourself in the 'shoes' of these characters. To wonder aloud about what they might have been thinking and feeling and doing in the midst of it all. To reflect on their own specific circumstances, roles, hopes, and fears. Their lives and the unwritten, potential impact that they may have actually had in the broader story. In order to engage the faint voices of those with lesser parts in the drama. On a far deeper and more meaningful level than ever before.

We should do so because *their* voices, however slight and faint, cry out to be heard. To be uncovered. Encountered. Considered. Honored. To be given the life that these voices deserve. In the process, your view of the stories will change. You'll change, as well. Thanks to the faint, but transcendent voices you took the time to hear for a change. When you truly listened.

Welcome to the Family

In the 2nd Testament Gospel of John, the previously crucified, but now recently risen, Jesus returned to his highly anxious disciples-in-hiding. Christ stood in their very midst and said, "Peace be with you. As the Father has sent me, so I send you." Then Christ breathed on them, imparting the Holy Spirit to each. And he stated that they would now have the power to forgive and retain the sins of others in their subsequent ministries. Many interpret this Biblical story as Christ's effort to conquer his disciples' unbelief and fear in the wake of his frightening and unexpected death. To empower them to do his work in the future. To actually send them out on their new mission. And to equip them for it through the Holy Spirit.

This story is largely about Jesus' 'gift' of the Holy Spirit prior to the Risen Christ's ascension to Heaven. But we can't truly understand the story in the absence of the larger context of the Holy Trinity. Three persons in one person, if you will. God, Christ, and the Holy Spirit. *God* is the source of all life and of all things. The grounding, the foundation, and the center. *Jesus Christ* is the incarnated and divine embodiment of God for us. Jesus reveals God and God's character to us all. The *Holy Spirit* is that which actualizes this embodiment. Makes it real. Translates it, if you will, in ways that can truly 'live' within our hearts—then sustains us, teaches us, and guides us in this light. This is the 'being' and the essence of the three members of the Holy Trinity in Christian faith. A truly 'together family'. From the very start. From the beginning. Not in sequence.

John's Gospel story of the Risen Christ's return is often read from the pulpit on Pentecost Sunday. Pentecost is part of Christianity's Easter celebration, encompassing a period of some weeks following Easter Sunday itself. Pentecost is one way of explaining to us the Holy Spirit as a member of the Holy Trinity. The Spirit as one divine 'person' within the three divine 'persons' comprising the Trinity. But we may miss the point entirely if we erroneously believe that the Spirit somehow 'became' in the moment of Christ's calling it forth. Even more importantly, we miss the point when we posit this: that the Holy Spirit was given to us for the primary purpose of enabling Christ's disciples and new believers to do something. To take action in spreading the message of Jesus.

When we read or preach from this story in John's Gospel, we should start with the all-important reference to Jesus, not necessarily the Holy Spirit. And it's important to state what the Risen Christ *didn't* do when he appeared to his surprised disciples. He didn't join these followers unannounced and exclaim, "I'm here! Look at me. I'm back from the dead. I did it. Just like I told you that I would." Jesus didn't spend time talking about all that he had been through. He didn't recount his birth, life, death, and resurrection stories. Further, the Risen Christ didn't preach to them about his beliefs. He didn't tell them parables. Nor did he give them detailed instruction about what was coming next. He didn't commission them to be priests and preachers in some mysterious line of succession. No. He simply came and stood in their midst. He showed them his wounded hands and his side to clarify his identity, but he didn't discuss these wounds at all.

What Christ *did* say is crucial here, though. He imparted this: "Peace be with you." In fact, he said it twice in the oft-read passage in John. Jesus wanted to emphasize it for sure. He didn't say peace '*go*' with you. He didn't say peace be with you in your work and your travels ahead. Or may peace equip you for the mission that I'm about to give you now. Or 'good luck because you'll need it, and I'm giving you a helper'. Instead, he simply said, "Peace be with you." Christ was talking about *being*, not doing, in the primary sense of the word. Simply being. Like when God told Moses, "I AM

WHO I AM" in response to Moses' query about God's name. 'Being' is the main thing here for Jesus, then.

Now, to be fair, Christ also said, "As the Father has sent me, so I send you." As such, he did send them in one sense of the word. But Christ's sending may be less about acting and doing here than we might otherwise think. Perhaps 'sending' relates principally to being *actualized* in Christ. Embodying God. Becoming members of the Holy Trinity through the Spirit. If this is the case, Christ's appearance before his disciples was not primarily a call to service. But, instead, an embodied call to God. A reminder to them (at a crucial, defining moment in time) of Christ's continued inner presence in them. Literally, of Christ's life-sustaining breath through the Spirit's actualizing power. A breath that was freely given through unbounded love and grace.

But what about Christ's words regarding, "Whose sins you forgive are forgiven them, and whose sins you retain are retained"? Many interpret this incorrectly as Christ having granted his disciples the power and authority to forgive human sinfulness. It's a problematic interpretation because only God can forgive sins. Further, sinfulness is less about our acts of immorality than about our separation from God. Anything that separates us from God is inherently contrary to God's loving plan for us. In this light, Christ's statement is, once again, a reminder of God's character. A reminder so powerfully embodied in Christ's own forgiveness of us all while he was on The Cross. If Christ could forgive this most grievous of sins, Christ can forgive *all* sins. To remove all sources of separation. For we are *all* invited to join in God.

In this Pentecost story in the Gospel of John, Christ breathed on his disciples. Through the Spirit, Christ gave them continued life. Literally, Christ's life-sustaining breath through the Spirit's actualizing power. A breath freely given as a gift through God's enduring love and grace. No action was required on their part, other than to trust in God's character. And to imitate Christ's 'being' to the best of their abilities by trying to embody God's character in their own lives going forward. Thanks to the ongoing sustenance of the Spirit. In other words, to become part of the Holy Trinity. A connected, welcomed member of God's family. Forever. Filled with peace. Living with peace.

God breathes on us, as well. We are also welcomed. But not simply to belong to something or someone. No. Much more than that. Instead, to live and breathe as a child, a person of God. One with God. In this sense, to transcend the seeming boundaries, limitations, and suffering of our respective walks of life. To 'be' as perhaps we've never been before. With minds and hearts and souls truly risen. Real, true, and amazing family.

Extraordinary Revelation

How do we know what we know? And how do we, as spiritual people, know about God? These foundational questions center on the notion of *Epistemology*. Thinking about epistemology goes back a long time. It's certainly not a new idea. It refers to 'meaning' and 'knowledge'. And it gets to the question of how we really come to discover and know what is true. And why we believe that things are true. How we justify something as truth versus just another opinion.

Now, as believers in the truth of God, we should constantly reflect on the Transcendent. And on God's ongoing role in our creation, sustenance, meaning, purpose, and direction. But to be honest, it's easy to take God for granted as always 'there' for us when things are going really well in our lives. Conversely, we can face painful periods of dryness and even silence in our God-thought. Like feeling separated from God's presence and actions when things aren't going well at all. If this happens, we might question, turn away, or give up. Or we may double-down in our efforts. We might pray harder. Pray more often. Pray louder. Or verbally cry out or even scream. In these times more than ever, we want God to reveal Godself to us in tangible, visible ways. "Come out, God. Show me that you're here, God. That you're real. That you're the truth."

But how does God reveal Godself, anyway? There are more ways than we could ever imagine, actually. Countess ways, in fact. Christian believers tend to rely primarily on the Bible. The Word of God. It's in reading, hearing, and preaching Holy Scripture that God (and God's work in history) is revealed to us. Christians also argue that God is revealed more specifically in the Bible through the incarnational and divine presence of God's own Son, Jesus Christ. 'God with us'. In fact, some denominational groups within Christianity argue that absolutely *everything* that we need to know about God and Christ is contained in the Good Book. Its words are infallible, unchanging, and inerrant.

While I don't deny the fundamental importance of the Bible as a primary source, I wouldn't limit myself to it either. For God began to reveal Godself to the universe long before the Bible was ever written. And before the human characters in the Good Book's stories were even born. God is, in fact, revealed through many sources, not just the Bible. God's revelation happens through nature and natural laws. God gives order to all things. For example, a physical phenomenon like gravity isn't an anomaly. When we let go of an object, it falls to the ground on earth. Amazingly, it does this every time. Reliably. Consistently. We can count on it. Because God made things that way.

That said, God's revelation in nature isn't simply a matter of establishing 'ways of operating'. No indeed. For God built unspeakable, unimaginable beauty into creation itself. One need only watch a sunset in the evening to witness the sheer artistry and magic of God's hands. Furthermore, it's not just nature that's revelatory. God is revealed in many other ways, as well. Revealed through our ability to think about God: our reason. Our capacity to rationally ponder God's purpose and presence in our lives. Through our shared human sense of morality. While this morality is strained in increasingly violent and hateful ways these days, we *do* have a shared moral compass. Certain things and actions are simply wrong. And we know it internally.

But that's not all. God is also revealed through our evolution as human beings. Via our ever-expanding ability to communicate, heal, innovate, invent, calculate, and generate information. Sadly enough, our track record in actually leveraging these evolutionary advances for the betterment of humankind is spotty at best. And we've used our technological advances in violent ways that imperil our very existence. The proliferation of nuclear, biological, and chemical weapons is only one frightening example among many. But that's on us, not on God.

So God reveals Godself in many, varied ways. We can therefore know God to a degree. Now, to be fair and realistic, we can't truly 'know' God in the way that we can know others—like our best friend, our spouse, or our child. For God isn't human and doesn't reside in our lives in the same way that our fellow humans do. Further, we can't 'objectify' God by putting God under a microscope to conduct a study. For that matter, we can't limit or constrain God either. We can't put God in a box and observe God moving around in it. Nor can we visually see God or describe how God looks. But we *can*, nonetheless, 'see' God revealed in multiple ways. By using our sources, our senses, our mind, and our capacity to wonder.

For while we don't ever meet God in the flesh, we can experience God in remarkable ways right here and now. And we can speculate about what kind of 'person' God really is. You know, God's characteristics. For example, we often describe God as all-knowing and all-seeing. Transcendent over us. Never changing. Ever constant. Sovereign. Some describe God as also immanent. This means that God is with us. At our side. Influencing and guiding us in our daily steps and walks. Changing us. But if we truly believe that God is immanent in our lives, there's a critical question to consider in this regard. Does the influence, change, and impact go only one way in God's revelation? From God to us.

Perhaps most people would argue 'yes'. As the Sovereign, Transcendent One, God is already perfect and complete. As such, God doesn't need us for God's own completion as part of God's immanent presence with us. Others believe otherwise though, as do I. Process Theologians hold that influence and revelation of an immanent God go *both* ways in our relationship with God. If we can experience and change through God, then God must simultaneously experience us, as well, as we reveal ourselves. And God changes in the process. This means that God is ever changeable. That God responds to us. Not just by acting on our behalf. God also transforms in the process of engaging and interacting with us. For to be in mutual relation demands nothing less.

But what does process theology mean on a practical level of daily human life? Well here's one thought: if God truly loves us, then God must be actually 'moved' by us, by our pain and sorrow, our sickness, our poverty, and our losses. God must somehow grieve for us and cry with us. Shed tears for us—then mix these tears with those streaming from our own eyes. Conversely, God must feel our exhilaration, jubilation, and laughter in life. Then join us in it. Be lifted by it. Additionally, if God is truly 'with us', then God must also listen to us. And be open to working within the spaces of our lives as revealed by us in order to help us. And be changed, Godself, as a result. Therefore, God is simply not an outside bystander, unmoved by all the action below on earth. Instead, God is an active, changing partner. Evolving as we do.

Sometimes it's hard to see God as involved, moved, and changing in the midst of our trials, though. I know from my own experience that it's brutally hard to witness the heartfelt cries of patients and families for healing. Tearful, fearful prayers of longing for God's healing mercies and miracles. Only to see the patient die a difficult, protracted, and painful death. It's also hard to see poverty, widening gaps in income, homelessness, violence, warfare, pandemics, and the dangerous warming of our climate without wondering where God is in it all. Who isn't moved by these urgent, pressing needs? So why isn't God changing God's tactics and approaches as the world changes so dramatically for the negative? Why isn't God doing something, already?

Some try to explain this inaction by noting that the 'ship has already sailed', if you will. That life's current messiness is really about our movement toward a predestined New World Order. In other words, the 'cake is already baked' for an Eschatological (future-based, end-times) community. One in which God will finally be in charge. Where God's will prevails once and for all. Gets done for a change. And those found worthy by Jesus will eternally inhabit the new order. Redeemed as Remnants of this earth. And welcomed into God's new Kingdom, now fulfilled in all its forever glory. So, in this sense, God's movement, involvement, and revelation are ultimately preordained and 'future' in nature. And so are we.

I would respectfully disagree on this front, I'm afraid. As previously discussed, God is revealed in many present ways . . . *today*. And God is moving within our current time and space in unscripted ways. Moved by us and via our own revelations to God. Moving within us. Moving alongside of us. Influenced by and engaged with us. And that's not even the whole of it. Because God is actively partnering with us in another important, but often far more subtle way: in our 'Moments'. Mutually-symbiotic moments, in fact. Now, in this form of partnership, God's revelation is admittedly less about what we actually consciously see and feel from God. And more about small, but significant, movements happening at an even deeper, more intricate 'moment' level.

Given their importance, what's the essence of *our* part in these moments? As human partners in this mutual revelation. To begin with, our moments aren't the same thing as our actions or the specific outcomes thereof. For while our actions in each moment do matter, the relative conditions of our respective 'hearts' matter far more. Why do we fill our moments with certain actions versus others? Why do we act as we do? And what intent are we really acting with? In other words, what's really going on inside us when we do this thing or that thing? What's actually driving the moment? So, these mutually revelatory moments are experienced at a heart and soul level.

But even if we 'get' this, there's another problem. Our human tendency (fostered in many religious traditions, by the way) is to keep trying harder. As such, it's tempting to continue building up as many possible moments as possible. In order to stockpile and individually relish in them. The more the merrier to keep this symbiotic, 'momentary' fellowship going strong. But doing so misses the point entirely. For it's not about the volume of our moments. It *is* about their quality in fostering *God's* plan. Our role is to nurture the soil in which potential 'moments' (ours and others) can germinate and sprout. Then to water, till, and weed the soil around them. To fertilize the 'moments'. To help them grow and flourish. To see them through as a partner with God right here and now.

If we look at 'moments' in this way, human spirituality is far less about our individual salvation and our eternal life in Heaven after we someday die. Instead, it's about the for-all-time, redeemable moments in our current lives. As such, it's possible that the real reward upon our earthly death isn't a ticket to the Pearly Gates after all. Instead, it's the 'heavenly moment' when we come to perfect understanding. About our prior living 'moments' that moved God along the way. That God joyfully redeemed in God's revelatory response. And we, in turn, experience unbounded joy in knowing that these moments are forever etched in God's plan. Perhaps this is our eternal 'Heaven' in our ongoing mutually revelatory presence with God.

Conversely, there's a darker side to the equation. Upon our death, we may also experience *this* while fully in God's Heavenly presence: a perfect understanding of the many moments that we wasted in our respective earthly lives. And come to know that God has now discarded these moments in response to our wastefulness in them. As a result, they will no longer exist or remain. Not redeemed in any way, not even a remnant of the now banished moments. And we learn this while simultaneously experiencing a deep, abiding sorrow and regret. Perhaps this is our eternal 'Hell' in God's revelatory presence.

This kind of Godly revelation 'in and of our moments' is therefore both present and future. It's about now and about later when we die. This revelation isn't 'General'—what some Christians call God's generalized, universal way of showing Godself. Furthermore, it's not 'Special' as defined by others of the Christian faith—meaning that God is revealed only to a few. To the chosen. The select. No. It's an *Extraordinary Revelation* by God. As Extraordinary Revelation, we can know this: that all things and all people are sacred. So is every moment that God provides and reveals as a possibility for us. Because each moment revealed can also be redeemed by God in time. In the end, nothing but nothing is outside God's reach and revelation. Not a single moment is wasted by God.

So seize this moment that God has just revealed to you. And the next. And the next. All of them. Seize them today. Tomorrow. And the next day for that matter. For while we may not understand the revelatory import of these moments now, we surely will someday. When God reveals it all to us perfectly in extraordinary ways!

'Quest'-ions for Prayer and Further Reflection

- Do you feel that God's peace and love are unconditionally with you each day? Or that they're somehow contingent on your every action, deed, or belief? Why and to what effect?

- In your own mind and heart, how is God actually 'moved' by your losses, suffering, setbacks, successes, and hopes? What does this say about your view of God? How helpful is this view to you in your spiritual journey?

- What truths and spiritual learning are you missing when you fail to deeply listen for the faint, but transcendent, voices of the poor, sick, lonely, and marginalized people of this world?

- What are the core, transcendent values and principles that undergird your human spiritual journey? How consistent are these values and principles with the realities of your specific worship communities, religious beliefs, and faith practices?

- How could you slow down a little and actually feel God's Spirit-breath in you more each day? What might you learn about yourself, others, and God in the process?

Our Quest for Meaning

Meaning:

- *Giving definition or expression to something*
  - *Our interpretation of a phenomena*
- *The truest intent or connotation of something*
  - *Finding significance and purpose in a thing*
- *Something's most significant content or importance*

Seemingly Contradictory

ONE RECENT EARLY EVENING, I saw the sun setting on the horizon of the western sky. The sun's brilliant orange and yellow colors melded almost mystically with the surrounding skies. Within this breathtaking picture, various tall, white, and billowy clouds stood like belligerent sentries in front of the sunset. These sentry clouds seemed to literally and visually resist taking on the colors of the background behind them. A loosing battle, to be sure, from the standpoint of the resistant clouds. But a winning one for me as witness to this skyward 'show'. For the multi-colored sky subsumed the clouds in a dazzling display of nature's grandeur and diversity.

When I subsequently looked to the eastern horizon, however, I witnessed something altogether different. But no less amazing. I saw a full moon just coming into view. Unusually clear and bright. The sky behind it was a dark blue, but not yet black. The moon was framed on its outside by a series of oblong clouds, extending sideways, not vertically, as in the west. The clouds were a deep red, mixed with a gray background. The eastern sky was simply spectacular. Wholly different than the western one, but equally spectacular nonetheless. More importantly, though, it felt quite special to see both day and night in the same sky. Simply by gazing at opposite horizons.

On this recent evening, I witnessed seeming opposites at the same time. For it wasn't really daytime anymore. Nor was it nighttime yet. It was actually an in-between time that we call 'dusk'. Dusk is humanity's way of placing a label or term of usage on the apparent opposites in the sky during the early evening hours. It's our means of creating a word to conform to our linear notion of chronological time. So we can maintain the clear, wholly distinguishable identities of day and night. In other words, dusk creates a linear time transition between these opposites. It makes us all feel safer. It makes the universe and our world appear more predictable. Orderly. On-time. But I don't particularly like arbitrarily separating things. Instead, I'd call what I witnessed on that recent evening as *both day and night*. Simultaneously occurring at the same time.

Proponents of day and night as opposites (ergo the need for dusk) fall into a category called *Dualism*. Dualistic thinkers segment phenomena into one pile or the other. For example, day is the opposite of night. Now, as far as categorizing something this basic goes, I suppose there's no real harm in it. We do it all the time, really. In sports, we have the home team and the road team. In movies, we have the leading lady and the leading man. In stand-up comedy routines, we have the straight guy and the funny guy. In law enforcement interrogations, we have the good cop and bad cop routine. In daily life, food portions are large or small. You get the idea. It's all part of our human effort to structure and organize things neatly.

But here's the problem. Our dualistic tendencies become far more troublesome in other, more substantive areas. Like when we apply dualisms to things such as morality. As is the case when we call someone right *or* wrong. Filled with light *or* darkness. Good *or* bad. Better *or* worse. This can be a dangerous way to see the world and each other, to be sure. For these dualisms divide, separate, and fragment things unnecessarily. And when accompanied by our judgment of others, it's spiritually worrying for several reasons.

First, simply tossing things or people into one pile *or* the other is an enormous oversimplification of life. For, in doing so, we grossly overgeneralize. And, as a result, things and people begin to lose their nuance. The many fine, intricate, and meaningful 'lines' of life's experiences are blurred or lost. Important and pleasurable variations of sight, sound, smell, touch, and taste begin to break down. In my own specific story, the evening skies that I recently witnessed would have forgone the subtly blending colors of grey, orange, red, and dark blue. Instead, the heavens would have been either black *or* white. And I would have missed something truly spectacular: the very rich diversity of this beautiful 'portrait' of nature at dusk.

Second, when we segment people into groups as opposites (and place value judgments on these opposites), we often discard the group that we value less. Because when people are either good or bad, we tend to demonize the bad ones. You know, 'in with the good, out with the bad.' Alternatively, we resort to creating hierarchies of goodness for people according to characteristics we deem desirable. The closer to good that you are, the better you are. The closer to bad that you are, the worse you are. You know, grading on the curve. Graded and rated, most typically, by those in positions of relative power. Political. Social. Economic. Class. Color. You get the idea, I'm sure.

If this dualistic practice is so distasteful, why do humans gravitate to fostering it? Perhaps we do so out of intellectual or emotional laziness. For, in truth, it's easier to categorize things as either 'this' or as 'that'. But there are other reasons too. Sometimes we do it out of our fear or anxiety. We're afraid of something or of someone. And the simplest way to deal with it is to demonize it. Cast it out as the enemy of good. Then we can rationalize how we talk about it with distain and disrespect each day. Or how we treat it when we experience that thing. Or when we meet the person we've neatly placed in that negative category.

As well, we gravitate to dualisms because we want to go along with current thinking. We don't want to rock the boat. Don't want to challenge the weight of inertia. Or we don't feel comfortable questioning past practices that have the weight of precedent. In other cases, we gravitate to dualisms because we need to feel superior. Maybe we're insecure at heart. And putting us at the top of the good pile makes us feel better about ourselves. Or about the political party we affiliate with. Or our social group. Or our religious institution and its underlying belief systems or dogmas. And on and on and on and on.

There's an old, well-worn saying about two competing versions of the truth that people hold. It states that the actual truth probably lies somewhere in the middle. In other words, we usually meet the truth in the middle of opposing stories. On the surface, this might seem to adequately address the problems of dualisms. For it overtly argues for compromise. If we move to the center of things, we'll probably find reality. And peace. Because, in the end, there surely must be elements of truth on both sides of the equation. Take a little of this. And a little of that. Join up in the middle.

However, there's a major problem with this approach. It fails to respect the authenticity of the very concept of opposites that dualists strive so hard to protect. It errs because it insists that, out of the two opposites, we have to find a common middle ground. Ironically enough, it ends up dealing with dualistic versions of the story by smashing most of both of these versions. So it's internally hypocritical. But worse yet, it ends up creating a new, agreed-upon, but perverse compromise version of 'truth' or 'good'—against which 'bad' is now judged going forward. Alas, old dualisms are simply replaced by new ones.

While some deal with dualisms by trying to find the middle ground, others try a different approach. They simply attempt to outwit the dualisms. We've heard the 1st Testament Biblical story of King Solomon, the wise ruler. You remember, the tale about two women in the same house who birthed children within just days of each other. One of the mothers rolled over on her child while she was sleeping and the baby died. The other mother accused the grief-stricken mom of switching the babies, so that the living baby was now with the grieving mother. And the innocent mother now had the wrong, deceased baby. She understandably felt aggrieved. King Solomon heard this complaint. And he decided on its merits by asking for his sword. He would resolve it by cutting the still-living baby in half. Then present half to each of the mothers, respectively.

One of the mothers begged Solomon not to do that. She said, "Please don't kill my son. Your Majesty, I love him very much, but give him to her. Just don't kill him." The other women replied, in turn, "Go ahead and cut him in half. Then neither of us will have the baby." Solomon listened intently and gave the baby to the mother who begged Solomon not to cut the baby in half. The King stated, "She is the real mother." Everyone was amazed at how wise Solomon was, and they praised his decision-making prowess.

It was a wise move in the moment, for sure. And lifesaving. But, as far as dualisms go, Solomon's actions still retained the notion that dualistic thinking is somehow good. For the King needed only be smart and clever enough to discern good *from* bad. He only needed to out-think the protagonists to ensure that 'goodness' prevailed. So we're left with dualisms intact here. Not so good in the end. Solomon 'dodged the bullet' but didn't wisely resolve the underlying dilemma of dualisms. So what if there's another way?

Yin and Yang might just be it. Yin and Yang is an idea borne of ancient Chinese philosophy. It asserts that seeming opposites may actually be complementary, balancing, and interconnected in reality. It demands far more work by us, to be sure. It requires that we look deeply into seeming opposites. To ponder them. To question their veracity. And to conclude, at times, that both might be true and complementary after all. It comes home to roost most often in our religious convictions.

Within the Christian tradition, for example, we fervently and uniformly believe that loving God and loving others are good. However, many simultaneously believe that loving one's self is bad. Selfish and self-centered in the very nature of this act. Therefore, we need to embrace the former. Conversely, we must discard the latter. The former is 'divine'. The latter is simply sinful. So 'in' with loving God and others. And 'out' with loving of self. This way of thinking is certainly not Yin and Yang. Further, it remains dualistic in every sense of the word.

Given the spiritual and religious importance of the 'loving self versus loving others' dualism more fully, let's dig deeper. At the outset, we'd probably agree that turning inward *solely* for the sake of doing so is dangerous. For when we attempt this, it's all too easy to become entirely self-obsessed. We're suddenly all about our own self-actualization. We can also turn into 'prisoners' of our own heads and hearts. In the process, we're prone to turning away from all things external. And as part of trying to find ourselves, we're likely to actually lose ourselves. That's right. Get lost. Internally disintegrate in a dualism, actually.

The other end of the dualistic spectrum is the idea of loving God and others at the expense of loving ourselves. If we're really honest with ourselves, this isn't terribly healthy either—however 'Christian' that it might sound in principle. For if we ignore self and live *only* for things external to us (even God and others), we can easily burn out. Become wholly dependent on things outside of us for our sustenance. We can violate proper human boundaries. We can morph into 'victims' when others don't reciprocate our own acts of loving kindness and generosity. We can also get angry with God when God doesn't reciprocate. Or answer our prayers and requests in a proper way. Or respond on time. We can, in turn, grow disenchanted. When this happens, we may withdraw. Disintegrate in a dualism, actually.

So, interestingly enough, we can spiritually disintegrate on *both* dualistic axes of the spectrum here. But if we ardently strive to force a compromise in order to meet in the middle, it's nothing more than smashing the two opposites together. What results isn't something new or better. No. It's only sausage. Like putting two wholly different kinds of meat into a grinder. And what comes out isn't anything special, either. It's only a bland combination of what once were two distinctive (even if extreme) flavors of meat. It's disintegrated, actually.

The notion of Yin and Yang helps us to avoid the disintegration of dualisms (and forced, murky compromises in the middle). It does so because it points us towards something different. It points us to *dualities* for a change. Unlike dualisms, dualities entail seeing two seemingly opposite, seemingly contradictory things as parts of a complex, interdependent life system. These apparent opposites exist at the same time in harmony, not in conflict or opposition. As a result, we strive to find truths not solely at either end of some arbitrary spectrum. And not in the middle for that matter.

So instead of extremes, opposites, compromises, and muddled mush, we could latch onto a bit of Yin and Yang for a change. Using our spiritual example of 'loving self versus loving others', we could actually do both on a guilt-free basis. We can do this while *also* understanding that the complementary aspects of self-love and projected-love, respectfully, necessitate our ongoing prayer, discernment, reflection, moderation, judgment, and intentionality. Our love of self, of God, and others can occur thoughtfully, simultaneously, and interdependently with a little effort on our parts. For these things aren't opposites.

Instead, they belong together in our spiritual exercise of meaning making in our respective lives. Truly together. Like day and night as 'one'. In the very same sky. Just like the two brilliant, beautiful horizons that I witnessed one early evening not long ago when I took the time to look up. On that night, the western and eastern horizons were seemingly contradictory. But, in reality, they were wonderfully complementary. Just like us . . .

The Exact Time Is . . .

It's 1:00 p.m. in the afternoon. In exactly 60 minutes, it will be 2:00 p.m. In precisely 24 hours, it will be the same time as now . . . but tomorrow, not today. Everything's marked by time as we currently define it. The clock advances in continuous motion. Each tick marks the slightest passage of time. One second. Then onto the next second. Then onto the next. Time is running, moving forward, seemingly linear. Neatly propelling us to the next thing in life. We look intently at our clocks, watches, or smart phones for the 'time'. We gaze at the numbers that we see in order to mark and control our progress today. This is what we call *Chronos Time*: human time as measured and managed by us in chronological days, hours, minutes, and seconds. It's a major part of how we find and measure meaning in our lives.

But what if there's another way to see time? To live within a different kind of time? Especially when something jolts us from those things that we typically mark by ordinary Chronos time. Like when lifelines become blurred. When existing ways of being, relating, communicating, and processing events become distorted or distended by a human crisis. Or, conversely, by our overt, conscious effort to break out of the 'prison of time' that we've created for ourselves and for others. In fact, the ancient Greeks were onto something in this regard. They coined the term *Kairos Time*. Instead of measuring time linearly, they also viewed it as referring to the exact 'right moment'. It's a measure of time that is potentially boundless and timeless. Perhaps incapable of measurement in our normal ways of thinking.

In Kairos Time, it's more about something of significant meaning that happens. Something qualitatively important to us, not quantitative relative to the time lapsed on our clocks. As qualitative in nature, Kairos Time is relational, connective, and transcendent. It can also be healing and transformational to our very souls, spiritually speaking. For unlike Chronos Time, our Kairos clock is less about *our* movement. Less about our actions or our progress. Less about our own control and influence. Less about the seconds that tick away on some clock or some watch. Instead, it's about the sacred moments *around and about* us. More about our being and our presence between each breath that we take. More of a noun than a verb, actually.

In order to break more fully into Kairos Time, we must also become a 'noun', as well. We have to slow down. Actually *stop* for a minute. Not in the Chronos sense of the word. But in a mindful way. Buddha was purported to have said, "Don't chase the past. Don't chase the future. The past is gone. The future hasn't come yet. But see clearly on the spot. See the object which is now. While finding and living in a still, unmoving state of mind." That's sound advice for our Chronos Time-obsessed culture today. But we have trouble heeding his words. And we're struck in 'Chronos'.

We're firmly encased in this mess for any number of reasons, I suppose. For starters, we're pressured and pressed. We're stretched and stressed.

We're acted on and distracted. Further, we try too hard at everything in life. Often letting 'great' get in the way of 'good'. Next, we believe everything that we think. And we believe too much of what we're told. But, perhaps most importantly, because we feel judged. We're bounded by time because we're afraid. Afraid of what others will think. And what we'll think about ourselves. How we'll be thought about if we don't make the most of our 'time'. When we live in judgment, we hold tightly to time in the traditional sense of the word. As if time is the last remaining air in a tank. And we're gasping for it, knowing that by doing so, we'll use it up even quicker.

When we judge ourselves or feel judged by others, we get swamped by our notions of time. More specifically, submerged in the dark abyss of the past and the future. When we look back in linear, Chronos Time, *to our past*, we swim in our guilt. We ask things like, "Why in the world did I do that? What was I thinking?" We judge our missteps, our mistakes, our regrets, and our failures. Sometimes we feel sorry for ourselves. Wallow in it, actually. Sometimes it's even worse, though. We feel shame. Shame for ourselves. Or shame for others. Shame is often followed by anger. Self-directed. Or directed outwardly. Directed sometimes with laser-like accuracy. Right on the target. But sometimes directed in some diffused, generalized way. With high collateral damage.

Conversely, we often look to *future* Chronos Time with fear. We do so with significant anxiety. We say things like, "What if things don't work out? What if I fail tomorrow?" And when we do, we get fixated on the worst possible outcome. We worry and we fret. We get terribly overwhelmed by it all. Overwhelmed by all the bad possibilities. Even though they're not even remote probabilities. But the more we worry, the more we actually 'set up' the potential for failure. For we unconsciously gravitate to the things that we think about most. In other words, our future-worry creates an efficient, but highly self-damaging and meaningless, self-fulfilling prophesy for us.

So when we judge or feel judged, we set our internal clocks to the past and/or the future. We obsess on either one or both simultaneously. And when we do so, we've lost the *present*. We're not here. Now. And how tragically ironic this is. For when all is said and done, the present is *all* that we really have. Right now. As Buddha said, the past is gone. The future hasn't come yet. Who knows . . . he might have also said this, "If you're not where you are right now, you're nowhere." He most likely didn't, actually. But it would have made sense.

Now to be fair, we *do* need a measure of Chronos Time. We have to actually *live* our lives in a temporal, sequential way to a degree. We have appointments and deadlines. Routines can be helpful and stabilizing in our lives. Meaning is time-bound to a small extent. But far too many of us live *exclusively* in this constricted sense of Chronos Time. And we're imprisoned by the judgment that often accompanies it. Regretting the past. Fretting the future. Living anxiously. All the time.

But there's another way. Kairos Time knows no single season. It knows no stopwatch. It knows no limits or limitations. Instead, it's grounded firmly in the Mindful, Meaningful Now. It's about moments right now. Moments that transcend our frail human notions of linear time. It's about the significance of this very moment, not about those from yesterday or the possible ones tomorrow. Because we can't experience anything of significance now if we're not actually 'here' right now. Present. Fully present in this moment.

So let's cover up our clocks every so often. Leave our watches at home at times. Quit checking the time for a change. And make time for some 'real time'. Kairos Time. Today. This Kairos second. This Kairos minute. How about now?

Shifting Sand . . . Shifting Time

In the Brazilian film, *House of Sand*, the leading character is a female who's been left widowed by an abusive, pioneering husband in a remote desert section of Brazil on the coast. She's now raising their little daughter alone, stranded together in relative isolation. By happenstance, she meets a traveling man who is, in turn, raising his own son by himself after his wife died during the birth of this child. The two end up living together in a simple hut in the shifting sands. The mother's daughter becomes increasingly restive and problematic as an adolescent, and the girl begs to escape this 'prison of isolation' in order to see the wider world. The mother agrees to her leaving home when military troops, who are passing through the area, allow the girl to join them en route to a Brazilian city located some distance away.

Many, many years later, the now-grown adult daughter returns home for the first time to the desert on the coast. She encounters her frail, elderly mother, now widowed and alone, sitting in the hut on the sand. The daughter has brought her mother a portable battery-powered radio and other artifacts of the current era—none of which the mother has ever seen. The daughter excitedly tells her mother that 'man' has just landed on the moon.

They look into the night sky and peer at the moon together. They contemplate the notion of 'time' as part of the imagined travel of the astronauts to the moon. The mother asks her daughter what these astronauts discovered there upon landing. The daughter responds somewhat despondently that all they found was sand. The mother reflects, then smiles broadly and says how nice that is.

In this powerful film, the daughter returned home from her search for meaning. She left the simple, isolated reality of her past in order to seek an understanding of life in the present, as it existed in the world of ideas, living, and reality. As the future unfolded at the end of the film, though, she found herself deeply disappointed by the moon landing. For she learned that time didn't actually slow-down for the astronauts. These space travelers simply came back older. Time marched forward, as normal, after all. Further, all they found on the moon was sand. Nothing more than sand.

However, for her mother, this meant something different altogether. The now elderly woman was reminded of something that had comforted her throughout her long life. The very sand that utterly surrounded her hut and her life (past, present, and future) was *also* omnipresent in such a distant and sought-after place as the moon. The mother's decision to remain in her simple life on the sand was affirmed. In turn, her search for meaning had traveled full-circle to the simplicity of the sand, itself. In many ways, the mother's past, present, and future had also melded together seamlessly in a time machine of blissful sameness.

The human notion of time is a messy, sandy, and complicated one, to be sure. Like the daughter in the movie, we often find ourselves arbitrarily separating time into past, present, and future. We do so in order to make sense of things. To cope. To move on. To survive. Or to simply forget. As people of faith, we also look to God to help us to understand and to compartmentalize time. To help us cope. To help us move on. To help us survive. Or to help us to simply forget. In time. However imperfectly, narrowly, and incompletely that we define it or even comprehend it.

As humans, we can realistically perceive time as *only* logical, linear, and sequential. Multi-dimensional notions could lie beyond our comprehension. At the same time, though, our healthy human wholeness depends, in part, on our thinking outside the sand box. For in reality, the notions of past, present, and future intermix and intertwine quite fluidly and creatively in a spiritual continuum of time that we call 'life' in our respective faith journeys. Like grains of sand. So we must, in turn, respond with openness and curiosity in thinking differently about time. Especially in the context of our spirituality.

Many faith traditions firmly believe and hold that God has acted to create this world. From nothing. Into something amazing, beautiful, and life giving. And that God has worked throughout past history to help shape it. But humanity has *also* influenced the past. We've purposefully and meaningfully shaped history in partnership with God. In fact, we've not only fashioned the past, but have learned something from it, as well. At least on those occasions when we've rationally exercised reflection, discernment, and openness. When we've actually grown from our history and applied it to what comes after. When we've done these things, *our past has helped to shape present.*

At the same time, though, our *present has also influenced the present.* For example, when we've turned to others in love and grace, we've set things in motion. We can't even begin to imagine the awesome power of our outward acts of kindness. We can only speculate as to how God has used them to change the world right now for the better. Leveraging our little ripples to make even bigger ones. In truth, our own inherent human limitations mean that we can only do a little in the great scheme of things. We are builders, not master architects or cosmic creators. But we can and should make a difference for others today. And we can live joyfully in knowing that we tried. So 'present' has shaped the present.

That's not the end of it, though. For *our present has also impacted the future.* When we've reached out in real love to others, we've helped them to build their own tomorrows. Better ones. Transformational ones. We've supported them in dreaming and realizing their own 'someday' visions. We helped to facilitate their self-empowerment. We've offered a guiding hand. We've witnessed their courage and humanity to others. We helped them keep the light burning. We've partnered respectfully to knock down barriers. We've offered an encouraging word. Sometimes, we've simply stood with and by them. At others, conversely, we've simply gotten out of their way. In all of this, 'present' has shaped future.

Lastly, *the future has influenced the present.* Our tomorrows profoundly impact today. Because of hope. There is no greater attribute of faith and spirituality than God's expectant, future hope. And when we act on the basis of this hope, we bring forth current, directed energy in our hearts and in those of others. For future hope, when accompanied by demonstrations of love, brings forth current possibilities. Future hope transforms the helplessness of oppression and suffering into the ever-present 'now' focus needed to overcome the daunting challenges before people. Into the steadfastness needed to persevere in faith today. Into the energy required to firmly grasp purposefulness today. Into the necessary power that transforms barren fields into a bountiful crop today. In these and many other ways, God's future hope has brought us real change *now*. Has shaped our lives today. Therefore, the future has helped to form the present. The hope and faith of tomorrow has blessed today. And continues to do so tomorrow, as well.

As in the Brazilian film, *House of Sand*, the sand beneath our feet is shifting. So is the concept of 'time' as we've explored it here. For past, present, and future are fluid. Intermixing. Intertwined. Mutually symbiotic. Mysterious. Complicated at times. We don't always learn from the past, to be sure. We sometimes lose the present when we 'live' solely in the past or in the future. And we squander God's gift of future hope when we don't let it fully energize real possibilities right now. Further, we can't stop the process of time any more than we can direct the winds or the swirling sand. Time keeps marching, however we define it, like small kernels of sand that drop slowly through an hourglass.

In this sense, we all live within our own respective hourglasses. These are our homes, of sorts. Our own 'huts', if you will. And our huts, as was the case in the Brazilian movie, are surrounded by sand. This sand, like time, is always under our feet. It's the *'past'* ground on which we've walked before. Further, this sand, like time, is in the air that we currently breathe—and is the *'present'* ground on which we draw our life source today. Finally, the sand, like time, is also blowing toward us from tomorrow. And it's doing so in ways that we can't sometimes fully see. For it's from the *'future'* in front of us.

Thus, the sands shift continuously underneath, around, and within us. However, this doesn't necessarily make our footing shaky or unstable. For the pliant sand, like time, is our grounding reality. And, as we've discussed, we must actively seek to understand our past, present, and future in the sands of time. And to gather meaning from them. But the elderly woman in the Brazilian film reminds us of this: we always return to the sand. It's the sand of true timelessness. Not timelessness in the sense of chronological chaos or blurred reality. But rather the seamless, interdependent, and mutually supportive nature of past history, the current present, and the future yet to come.

Humankind may travel yet again to the moon. In the future. As we did in the past so many times before. When we do, we'll bring home more samples. Of sand. We'll look back. We'll rejoice in the present moment. And we'll muse upon the next trip someday thereafter. For the shifting sands on the moon and on our earth are inexplicably intertwined and timeless. In the past. Right now. And forevermore. What a future, indeed.

The Joy Beneath the Surface

The leaves that we rake and clear away each autumn lay idly in small piles and rows at the edges of our properties. By November or early December, the brilliant red, orange, and yellow colors of the leaves have faded to a dark, almost colorless shade of brown or grey. Like the nuts and twigs that have also fallen from lofty branches in the autumn winds, the leaves are slowly decomposing within the soil beneath them. It all represents a 'death' of sorts, I suppose. But its irony is that this 'death' brings new life—quietly and invisibly by nourishing the ground for the spring that will soon arrive. As such, it's easy to be deceived by the outward lack of color and life during those cold winter months. For much is actually going on under the surface of things while the soil appears to simply sleep.

Joy is a lot like that, I imagine. But we throw the word 'joy' around with an almost casual indifference to its true meaning at times. We carelessly fuse it with other words, such as happiness, pleasure, enjoyment, elation, and cheerfulness, to name a few. And we prescribe myriad benefits to these supposedly similar words in our daily lives: greater energy, calmness, openness, and even spirituality. Those are good outcomes, to be sure, whatever the source they stem from. But joy is not the same as happiness. Nor is it the same as pleasure. Further, joy facilitates profound spiritual outcomes that other 'like' emotions simply cannot. As such, we confuse true joyfulness with ancillary notions to our own detriment.

For those other things are impermanent, contingent, dependent, unsteady, and perhaps even unrealistic. What's more, they imply taking an action on our part, as if we need to do something in order to keep all the happiness going. Or they demand our constant vigilance and protectiveness. In order to stop external negativity, setbacks, stress, losses, or disorder from creeping into our lives. You know, ruining our good times. Using my opening seasonal analogy, it's as if we have to desperately and tightly hang onto the branches of the tree . . . lest our green leaves wither and fall to the ground as happiness lost.

Here's the thing. True joyfulness is far more inclusive than happiness. Joy transcends happiness. In fact, it's possible to have the former without the latter. For joy works beneath the surface, ever-nurturing the soil. Even on the coldest, darkest, and unhappiest days of our lives. It does so *if* we'll cultivate this joy each and every day. Yes, we have a part to play here. We cultivate meaningful joy when we take time to actively use our senses. To utilize our sight, hearing, touch, smell, and taste. We cultivate joy when we regularly pause or stop—then take a deep breath. When we get outside our heads for a change. Get out of our homes. Go outside. Take a short walk, even on the coldest days of winter in order to seek a new and different perspective and meaning.

That's not all. We cultivate joy when we practice thanks and gratitude, even in situations where it's difficult and challenging. We cultivate joy when we work to release our hurts each day. When we affirm ourselves and affirm others as inherently worthy. When we pray and meditate. When we stay close to God. When we come to peace with the many unknowns, uncertainties, and unsolvable mysteries of our earthy existences. When we plan less and trust more. When we surround ourselves and surround others with love. Lots and lots and lots of love.

All these things cultivate joyfulness. But perhaps nothing does so more than simplifying our respective lives. Living 'less large', if you know what I mean. For 'smaller' can be 'larger' as joy goes. Think deeply about a recent, wonderful day that you've experienced. It may have entailed nothing more than sitting outside. When you watched the brilliance of a clear, star-lit night. Or gazed upon a field of wild flowers. As these flowers literally danced to the music of a summer's breeze. Or when you cherished a bowl of delicious cold ice cream on a hot day. Or hugged someone whom you loved. Or listened to the infectious laughter of children as they ran and played.

Then ask yourself this: how much did these truly special times of joyfulness really cost you? How complicated was it to experience the resultant deep and lasting joy? How much advance planning did these experiences really require? How much stress and worry were involved? And what did you actually 'accomplish' in the act of feeling so joyful? I suspect that the profound joy that you experienced actually cost very little. It probably required relatively little planning. Involved little sacrifice on your part.

Instead, these experiences were far more about your 'being' fully in the moment as you enjoyed the sheer wonder of simplicity entailed in them.

Further, you experienced this joy *within* the context of your own routines, limitations, and even your own sufferings. Perhaps in spite of those things. Most importantly, though, the best part of joy you enjoyed came from the 'inside out'. It came from *within* your heart, even if you seemingly experienced things outwardly. And because of this inward centering, your joy won't ever leave you. It remains with you. Even if invisible to the naked eye. Like the leaves beneath the ground's surface on a winter's day, true joyfulness continues to quietly, but powerfully, work 'inside'. Work to meaningfully nurture your spirit and your soul. To bring new life when winter turns to spring. This is truly hopeful. This is truly joyful.

Revolutionary Change

It's a time of rapid innovation. We've witnessed significant advancements and innovations in science, technology, communications, transportation, industry, organizations, and manufacturing processes. We can generate and transmit a vastly greater volume of information—and can do so far more quickly than ever before. We see a virtual onslaught of new, novel management practices with respect to where and how we work together. Public health and medicines are lengthening average life spans, while curing previously incurable ailments. Many people are experiencing higher standards of living. Conversely, others are being displaced from their jobs due to the many changes now underway.

What's more, work is becoming increasingly specialized, with 'winners' and 'losers' in the process. Some regions are facing labor shortages, while others see high and chronic unemployment. Wealth is increasingly concentrated in fewer people—as the gap between the 'haves' and the 'have-nots' continues to widen. Economic uncertainty is hurting the economy. We're witnessing an unmistakable population shift from rural to urban areas, with all of its attendant benefits and challenges. Finally, there are growing disparities around population growth, with some geographic areas experiencing unsustainably high levels . . . while others are actually losing people.

As you read this description, you'd be correct in dating these developments as relatively current. The last decade of the 20th Century (and the first few of the 21st) are notable for their seismic transformations. These changes are dramatic, dynamic, and perhaps even unsettling for many. They're all too real in our lives today. What's also real, however, is this: the *same* things could have been said during the 2nd Industrial Revolution many, many years ago. This historical period, roughly from 1870 to 1915, was characterized by highly similar phenomenon. It was equally revolutionary in its change. And it was equally unsettling to the people living in that era past.

In fact, the monumental challenges in navigating change are seemingly timeless. In the Bible's 1st Testament, we learn of King Solomon, son of King David. Upon David's death, Solomon assumed the throne. Solomon prayed to God for wisdom, discernment, and insights—not for riches, a long life, or the vanquishing of his enemies. This pleased God, and God granted the things that Solomon requested. The King ruled over all of Israel for forty years. His wisdom was renowned. He shepherded the building of the Temple, his palace, and a vast fleet of ships for far-reaching commercial activities. He conscripted thousands of residents to complete these ambitious, difficult projects. He acquired great multitudes of horses and chariots. Needless to say, a great deal of change was afoot within the kingdom under Solomon's rule.

For all of Solomon's wisdom, you'd think he'd have figured out the whole change thing. But, sadly enough, he hadn't. And he unduly burdened his people. He turned his back on God by taking many wives . . . then allowing the worship of idols. When Solomon subsequently died, his son, Rehoboam succeeded him. Rehoboam was probably 'way in over his head' upon assuming the throne. More likely than not, he was poorly informed or even clueless as to the substantial, negative impacts already created by his father's arduous and taxing change agenda. And things didn't get better from there, either.

Rehoboam heeded some bad advice to keep the too-rapid pace of change going strong. He ignored far wiser counsel to slow things down in order to give his fatigued people some change relief. And, in so doing, he set in motion the subsequent fracture and break-up of the Kingdom. In the end, it wasn't a good case study on change management. By either Solomon or Rehoboam. Like father, like son. The apple didn't fall too far from the tree, I'm afraid. A couple of 'not-too-wise-guys', as it turns out.

So change is hard. And it's always been difficult for us as human beings. No one really likes change. Except, perhaps, a baby with wet diapers. But why do we struggle so mightily with the very notion of change? It's largely because we prefer the comfort of the status quo. We feel far safer in the midst of equilibrium. It's more secure. Further, change is confusing and disorienting to us. The nature of change, itself, is one of dynamic movement. It implies navigating the unknown. And we often fear that. Change also brings new people, places, and things into our lives. It breaks up our established ways of thinking, being, acting, and relating. It demands that we do these things much differently than ever before.

This is particularly difficult when we don't understand the reason for the change before us. When everything appears to have been working just fine before the change was 'forced' on us. By someone from the outside who doesn't really 'get us'. And in the absence of a 'burning platform' that demands that we 'jump' now. Maybe most importantly, though, change is hardest when it's accompanied by human loss. When it requires that we leave things behind. That we say 'goodbye'. That we grieve what is gone. It can be a hardship, to be sure.

As spiritual beings who continuously seek meaning, we react to change in a variety of ways. How we respond is often influenced by the degree of 'control' that we feel that we have in the face of change. But, under *any* circumstance, change brings forth a wide range of human feelings. At times, we respond by denying the need for the change itself. At others, we outwardly and sadly long for the good old days. Or we choose to resist the change. To overtly push against it. To sabotage it at every turn. Alternatively, we 'snipe' at it from behind our protective 'wall'. Use guerilla tactics. Like passive-aggressive behavior at its worst.

On a more positive trajectory, we sometimes engage with the change. At least tentatively at first. To put our toe in the water. We're likely to be cautious and risk-adverse at the outset, though. Fearful about too fully embarking on the change in its early stages. That said, a few of us go even further. And choose to *fully* embrace the change. Actually enjoy it. Become energized by it. See it as an opportunity to stretch and grow, and not as a threat. But, if we're completely honest, most of us don't fall into this camp. Because it's simply too hard for us. So we 'dig-in' our heels to one degree or another. Or only tentatively, pensively engage with it. We keep our head down, hoping that the change will pass harmlessly over us at some point.

Given the persistence (and difficulty) of human change, there's no shortage of 'experts' willing to share solutions to it. To help us navigate through it. Models and systems abound, in fact. We can read books about it. We can buy programs to help us. We can attend seminars. We can seek advice at every turn. We can cry on the shoulders of our families and friends. As spiritual people seeking meaning, we can also learn about the stages of change. Then can plot our respective statuses in this step-by-step process.

As we do so, we often double-down on our efforts. Work harder and harder to progress sequentially along the change curve. To successfully get to the end of it. Then get over it. Along the way, we try to actively communicate with others. And we hope that others will be honest with us about it. We strive to get more organized. We plan more. Do more. Try more. All in the name of pushing through the change. To restore our sense of equilibrium, wherever it may now lie in our post-change world.

There's a problem with this strategy, though. Because change isn't something that we ever really get through. Isn't something that we conquer or get behind us. No. In fact, change *is* 'the thing'. Consequently, we find human meaning in change only when we increase our innate *capacity* to thrive within the change itself. To live more fully and continuously within the change space. If so, what does this require? First, we have to become 'change visionaries'. Always anticipating. Actually and actively seeking out change. And, as part of this, we must be fully centered in who we are. We accomplish this by defining ourselves in a better, healthier way. Not by our externally judged accomplishments, achievements, possessions, wealth, and looks. But according to our intrinsic, inherent, inner selves. By finding meaning not as the world so often does. But from our insides.

Second, we must hold onto things far less tightly than ever before. And more fully embrace impermanence in this regard. Now to be fair, we *should* foster as much healthy, stable external constancy as possible in areas such as family, faith, friendships, and self-fulfillment. But the truest, best constancy ultimately stems from our trust in *ourselves*. And our willingness to invest in 'us'. We invest in ourselves when we're open. When we're willing to look into our very own souls. And to be honest about why we're afraid of change. About our own felt-insecurities and the reasons for them. About exactly where we need to grow and stretch in this regard—then get help in these spaces. In order to more fully thrive in times of change.

Third, we have to get clearer on our overarching goals. About what gives us our truest meaning and purpose in life. About what should matter most to us. These things should transcend much of the change fury around us. They should ground us in something 'greater' than us. Balance us in ways more powerful than the fickle winds of change. Further, when we're grounded in transcendent goals and meaning, we change how we respond to change.

We respond in more resilient, healthier, and constructive ways. We become more positive and optimistic about the change. Further, we're able to take a longer view of things. We can measure our progress, our milestones, our successes, and our continued learning 'edges'—irrespective of the pressures and problems at the moment. Of course, we must be appropriately pliant. For our grounding sources of meaning may change to a degree over time. But standing on our 'vision' is a far more stable platform for succeeding in constant change. And thriving in change is truly possible, however challenging it may seem.

In the end, change has been a constant part of 'being' human. What was true in Biblical times was also true in the 19th and 20th Centuries. And it's still true today. In fact, it's always been so. Change is ever-present. For, as previously noted, change *is* the 'thing'. It's not simply a transition between 'past' and 'future'. It's not a time between what 'once was' and what 'will be'. Nor is it a period of unfreezing before subsequently refreezing things. Therefore, change isn't temporal. It's not incremental, either, for that matter. In fact, it's revolutionary. We, in turn, become revolutionary when we learn to more fully engage with change, not simply muddle through it. When we grow our capacity to actually live within change with greater faith and hope. In a revolutionary kind of way, of course.

Re-Awakening our Inner Child

"Grow up! Act your age! Start thinking like a grown-up for a change! Quit acting like such a little child!" We've all heard these things. Perhaps they've been directed toward us from time-to-time in our respective lives. The worst part of hearing this stuff isn't that it makes us feel bad. Instead, it's that we actually believe this advice in the first place. Then we internalize these things in our minds, hearts, and souls. Then we become 'old souls' well before our time. And not in a good way.

Being the 'grown up' all the time starts early in our lives. It can be subtle or overt. Can come on slowly or all at once. Disguised or in our faces. For many, though, it's sneaky. It often begins as a thin veneer that incrementally covers us as we move through childhood. It subsequently becomes a hardened body cast as we grow older. Not a temporary, plaster one like when we broke our arm or our leg. No. A permanent one. And not even a cast, actually. But a mummification. All wrapped up in gauze and glue. Then covered with hardened concrete that doesn't come off. So we're all grown up. And we're all encased.

The movies *Home Alone* and *Home Alone 2* are family classics. In each film, a young boy, Kevin, is left alone over the Christmas holidays. In the first movie, he's all alone at home while his family has jetted off to France. In the second movie, he becomes inadvertently abandoned when he gets separated from his family on the wrong plane. He flies to New York City. His family flies to Florida. In both movies, Kevin is 'home' alone. On his own. Flying solo. Fending for himself over Christmas.

In each movie, Kevin falls prey to two bad guys. In the first film, these guys are out to burglarize his home. In the second, they're out to get him. In both movies, Kevin plots to confront these criminals by using elaborate tricks that he's creatively 'engineered'. And he does stifle them for a time. But in each film, the two thugs ultimately trap him. And, each time, Kevin is rescued by an adult. In the first movie, Kevin is saved by his neighbor Old Man Marley. Marley has been dubbed by Kevin's older brother as the 'South Bend Shovel Slayer'. The old man is erroneously rumored to have murdered his own family and neighbors years ago with a snow shovel. In the second film, Kevin is rescued by the Pigeon Lady in New York City's Central Park. The Pigeon Lady spends nearly all of her time reclusively in the park feeding the birds.

Importantly, both Old Man Marley and the Pigeon Lady play the role of Kevin's ultimate protectors and saviors. Kevin's parents, on the other hand, have somehow lost track of their child. Not once, but two times. In turn, they play the role of frantic, anxious, and guilt-ridden adults. They spend both movies desperately trying to overcome their own mistakes by getting back to their lost son. And somehow trying to make it right again. But the real 'star' of these two movies isn't Kevin's parents or the other adults. Not even close. *Kevin* is the undisputed star. His own role takes center-stage through his many humorous lines, his antics, and his clever ways of getting into and out of trouble.

But, more symbolically, his role matters most for what he offers to the adults in the film . . . and all of us by extension. For Kevin's greatest contribution is simply being a child. His innocence. His unanticipated insights. His creative thinking. His genuine openness to the world. His unabashed curiosity. His human connection with others. His ability to reconcile things and people. His ability to heal others. His ability to forgive in a childlike way. And his capacity to impart truth to adults. You know, to the people who have already grown up. An interesting role-reversal, to be sure.

In the first *Home Alone* movie, Kevin offers healing to a stranger in a church. When he inadvertently sees (and briefly sits with) Old Man Marley in the church pew. In this scene, Kevin-the-child becomes a priest-confessor, of sorts, to Marley. When Marley confides to Kevin that Marley no longer sees his estranged son and his family. That Marley isn't involved in his granddaughter's life anymore because of this emotionally tragic riff. That Marley can't even remember what caused the argument to begin with so many years ago. But the old man never calls his son nonetheless. Because he's afraid that his son might not answer the phone.

As a result of this estrangement, Marley is feeling deeply alone. And feeling deeply sad. Interestingly enough, Kevin uses *his own* child-like story of his fear of his home's dark basement in order to help the old man. In essence, Kevin tells Marley to do what he did. Simply turn on the lights. And he encourages the old man to call his son. To get over his fear about doing so. For if Marley tries to call and it doesn't work out, at least he'll know for sure. Then he can move on with his life instead of staying afraid. Out of the mouths of children . . .

In *Home Alone 2*, the Pigeon Lady invites Kevin to watch a concert from a loft high above Carnegie Hall one night. The lady opens up to Kevin about her losses, her many disappointments and regrets, and the tragic setbacks in her life. She is homeless and lonely. Kevin promises to be her friend if she needs one. At the conclusion of the film, Kevin runs from his hotel to Central Park, where she is feeding the birds. He gives her one of two turtledove ornaments that he has. Kevin does so as a tangible measure of his prior promise to be her friend. He'll keep the other one—meaning that they'll each have something to remind themselves of about the other person. He tells the Pigeon Lady, "I won't forget you. Trust me." They hug each other. In this touching scene, Kevin offers something far greater than an ornament. He gives himself wholly in friendship to another. He intrinsically knows the thing that matters most of all to her. Out of the mouths of children . . .

And what about the adults in the two films? They're characterized, for the most part, by anxiety, guilt, distraction, loss, stress, regret, fear, and loneliness to one degree or another. To be fair, some of them *do* provide Kevin with a measure of safety and protection. But in most every other way, it's the adults who are the most emotionally needy. It's the adults who are most lost and alone. Conversely, Kevin is the one supposedly 'trapped'. But he's the *only one* having any real fun. Kevin is the *only* character having an adventure. Now he is in some danger, to be sure. But he is joyfully finding himself (and some true Christmas holiday meaning) in the process of taking some risks. Creatively thinking outside the box. And purposefully stretching himself along the way.

While risking a tenuous parallel here, here's a question to consider: how do *our* lives as spiritual people mirror those of the characters in the films? For Christians, what can the life of Jesus teach us about awakening our inner child as we continuously seek purpose and meaning? As a people of faith, Christians celebrate and worship Jesus. We focus much of our attention on Christ's death and resurrection. To a degree, we also focus on Christ's ministry, his sayings, and his miracles. We don't, however, focus nearly enough on his birth. We talk about it only around Christmas time. During Advent. And on Christmas day for the most part.

But in the process, many of us tragically forget the *greatest* miracle about Jesus. It wasn't just having God 'with us' as Emmanuel. It wasn't just the healings and the feeding of the thousands. It wasn't just his calming the tumultuous seas. No. It was that God actually came to us as an Innocent Child, the baby Jesus Christ. Who was born into relative poverty within a damp and dark cave. Long before Christ became the sacred bearer of Good News, hope, wisdom, and revelation, he was first a child. In this sense, then, we risk worshipping and celebrating the wrong thing when we turn the focus away from the 'child in Jesus'.

To be fair, we know very little about Christ's childhood. For the Bible is largely silent on this score. We *do*, however, know that Christ got lost as a small boy, separated from his parents one day. Mary and Joseph frantically searched for Jesus, only to find him in the Temple. Where the Christ-child was teaching the elders and adults. Where Jesus was sharing his wisdom, ideas, and insights with them. Sound familiar? While trying to avoid a too-close parallel here, Kevin was doing a tiny bit of the same thing in the *Home Alone* movies, however un-divinely so. Out of the mouths of children . . .

Given this, what if the most important thing about Jesus Christ wasn't his doing amazing things with bread and fish? Wasn't about his miracle cures. Or even his awaking people from the dead. But rather that Jesus mattered *most* by the wonder and adventure of his own 'inner-child'. Christ cut to the chase in ways that the more 'mature' adults around him had long since forgotten to do. He wasn't afraid to speak up concerning what God had instilled in his heart. Wasn't afraid to 'turn on the lights' in his life or in the lives of others. To think outside of normal, customary ways of thinking. To reinterpret the world for a refreshing change.

Furthermore, Christ's greatest gift was (and is) the 'inner-child' that Jesus wants us to have *within*. Not to carelessly give away or to discard in our hurry to grow up. Or to move on from as soon as possible. Or to 'get real' in life in the spirit of mature adulthood. No. It's a gift to wondrously cherish: our 'inner-child' in our deepest recesses. If we let go of our felt-need for safety, protection, relief from pain, and risk aversion in our respective lives. To become far less fearful and anxious. To relinquish our need for certainty. Or our continuously seeking all the stuff that 'grown-ups' are supposed to chase.

If we hold more dearly onto this gift of our 'inner-child', we'd anxiously scurry about far less. We'd spend far less time running to catch planes, cabs, and airport limousines. We'd spend far less effort running away to far-flung places in order to get away from it all. Or to frenetically race back 'home' to frantically search for someone lost. For the 'someone lost' is probably us anyway. We're the ones left home alone. What we're desperately trying to find is our innocence. The very innocence that we tragically pushed away so early in our respective lives.

We don't need adult protection to find this innocence again. We don't require Old Man Marley to save us with his snow shovel. And we don't need the Pigeon Lady to call all the birds to our rescue. In the innocent spirit of Kevin in the *Home Alone* movies, we *could* eat a lot of ice cream and pizza. We could jump on the bed. Order room service. Watch old movies. Sing loudly and unabashedly at the bathroom sink. Imagine. Explore. Create. Share a turtle dove ornament with a friend. And turn on the lights in the dark, unused basements of our souls.

Perhaps most importantly though, we could bring forth the Baby Jesus in each of us. To let the spirit of *his* childhood, the very childhood that we know so little about in the Bible, to come into us more fully, freely, and wonderfully. To allow Jesus to graciously 'gift' us with a fresh, more fully innocent sense of meaning in our lives. And to get playfully 'lost' for a change. Only to be truly found for the first time ever.

'Quest'-ions for Prayer and Further Reflection

- In what ways do your current beliefs cause you anxiety, emptiness of meaning, anger, disappointment, or even disbelief at times? Why?
- How does the rapid, continuous change around you impact your life most significantly? How well are you really coping with it and why?
- How can you draw deeper meaning and joy in your life, transcending the inevitable 'ups and downs' of your daily walk?
- In what ways do your past and your expectations for the future impact you right now? How can you use the past and an expectant future more positively to support you spiritually?
- How might you live your spirituality and your life in a more balanced way—to include more equal elements of believing, thinking, acting, feeling, and relational spheres of 'being' . . . instead of simply 'either-or'?

Epilogue: The Quest

To take a quest is to decide. To make a choice. To resolve to do.
To push further than we've ever done before. To try something radically new.
But when we step out, one thing's for sure. Obstacles will abound. All around.
There'll be rickety bridges and moats and pits. And mud and dust and dirt.
We cross rough terrain. And sandy dunes. With rocks and boulders. Ledges too.
We'll face dragons and demons. Some from the outside. Some from within.

So there's not an easy part. Not a single one. It's not for the meek-at-heart.
For a quest is, by its very nature, an unsettling thing. We cannot quest in-place.
Because to quest is to ask. To question. To examine. To investigate and invest.
Not simply in our minds, but in our hearts and souls and spirits and bodies.
To push every boundary that we've ever known. To go beyond what's known.
To find new things. To find new meaning. To even find new words. Like 'quest'.

A quest is a noun and an adjective. But it's also a verb. An active verb at that.
A quest is a mission. A search. A voyage. A pilgrimage. And a journey. A *noun*.
A quest is adventurous, joyous, frightful, risky, long, and tiring. An *adjective*.
To quest is to hunt. To pursue. To seek. To travel. To search. To stretch. A *verb*.
That's what makes our human quest so great. For it's so many 'words' in one.

Our quest helps us to know who we are inside. It defines us in a way.
And it describes us as a person. It illustrates our progress. And how we change.
But most of all, it sets our motion. As beings worth living. And actively growing.
A noun, an adjective, and a verb. Our quest defines, describes, and moves us.

Our quest is a defining, unbinding moment. A moment of truth. Worthy of a call.
And the call is out. The quest is on. It's on for sure. So take the step. Step *out*.
For stepping back is to lose one's soul. And standing still is to lose one's place.
For what it's worth, only one step matters. The one that moves forward.
Unbinding. Questing. And truly being. Now and perpetually so.

With Infinite Gratitude . . .

TO ALL THOSE WHO have joined me in the many 'travels' of my life. To all who have supported, encouraged, guided, blessed, and loved me. To all who've inspired and challenged me to write three books in the past few years. Who've been 'present' for and to me during this chapter of my life. Who have believed in me, even when requiring them to think outside the normal 'box' of authoring books such as those I've written. Who've invested spiritually in me over time, both inside and outside the confines of formal ministry. Who have been true, authentic friends to me at home, work, and play throughout my entire life.

But my infinite gratitude extends most joyfully and fully to God—who has given me life, grace, inspiration, wonder, courage, and persistence. Next to God, I thank my wife, Carmen, most of all. For Carmen is my earthly soul mate, my fellow traveler, and my fellow seeker. She is the one with whom I walk the earthly trail ahead. Sharing hopes for more journeys and adventures to come in our future together. Along the way. On our Quest.

www.ingramcontent.com/pod-product-compliance
Lightning Source LLC
Chambersburg PA
CBHW072135160426
43197CB00012B/2117